SharePoint Online Office 365 Complete Self-Assessment Guide

The guidance in this Self-Assessment is based on SharePoint Online Office 365 best practices and standards in business process architecture, design and quality management. The guidance is also based on the professional judgment of the individual collaborators listed in the Acknowledgments.

Notice of rights

You are licensed to use the Self-Assessment contents in your presentations and materials for internal use and customers without asking us - we are here to help.

Trademarks

D1663639

Table of Contents

About The Art of Service

The Art of Service, Business Process Architects since 2000, is dedicated to helping stakeholders achieve excellence.

Defining, designing, creating, and implementing a process to solve a stakeholders challenge or meet an objective is the most valuable role… In EVERY group, company, organization and department.

Unless you're talking a one-time, single-use project, there should be a process. Whether that process is managed and implemented by humans, AI, or a combination of the two, it needs to be designed by someone with a complex enough perspective to ask the right questions.

Someone capable of asking the right questions and step back and say, 'What are we really trying to accomplish here? And is there a different way to look at it?'

With The Art of Service's Standard Requirements Self-Assessments, we empower people who can do just that — whether their title is marketer, entrepreneur, manager, salesperson, consultant, Business Process Manager, executive assistant, IT Manager, CIO etc... —they are the people who rule the future. They are people who watch the process as it happens, and ask the right questions to make the process work better.

Contact us when you need any support with this Self-Assessment and any help with templates, blue-prints and examples of standard documents you might need:

http://theartofservice.com
service@theartofservice.com

Included Resources - how to access

Included with your purchase of the book is the SharePoint

Online Office 365 Self-Assessment Spreadsheet Dashboard which contains all questions and Self-Assessment areas and auto-generates insights, graphs, and project RACI planning - all with examples to get you started right away.

How? Simply send an email to
access@theartofservice.com
with this books' title in the subject to get the SharePoint Online Office 365 Self Assessment Tool right away.

You will receive the following contents with New and Updated specific criteria:

- The latest quick edition of the book in PDF

- The latest complete edition of the book in PDF, which criteria correspond to the criteria in...

- The Self-Assessment Excel Dashboard, and...

- Example pre-filled Self-Assessment Excel Dashboard to get familiar with results generation

- In-depth specific Checklists covering the topic

- Project management checklists and templates to assist with implementation

INCLUDES LIFETIME SELF ASSESSMENT UPDATES

Every self assessment comes with Lifetime Updates and Lifetime Free Updated Books. Lifetime Updates is an industry-first feature which allows you to receive verified self assessment updates, ensuring you always have the most accurate information at your fingertips.

Get it now- you will be glad you did - do it now, before you forget.

Send an email to **access@theartofservice.com** with this books' title in the subject to get the SharePoint Online Office 365 Self Assessment Tool right away.

Purpose of this Self-Assessment

This Self-Assessment has been developed to improve understanding of the requirements and elements of SharePoint Online Office 365, based on best practices and standards in business process architecture, design and quality management.

It is designed to allow for a rapid Self-Assessment to determine how closely existing management practices and procedures correspond to the elements of the Self-Assessment.

The criteria of requirements and elements of SharePoint Online Office 365 have been rephrased in the format of a Self-Assessment questionnaire, with a seven-criterion scoring system, as explained in this document.

In this format, even with limited background knowledge of SharePoint Online Office 365, a manager can quickly review existing operations to determine how they measure up to the standards. This in turn can serve as the starting point of a 'gap analysis' to identify management tools or system elements that might usefully be implemented in the organization to help improve overall performance.

How to use the Self-Assessment

On the following pages are a series of questions to identify to what extent your SharePoint Online Office 365 initiative is complete in comparison to the requirements set in standards.

To facilitate answering the questions, there is a space in front of each question to enter a score on a scale of '1' to '5'.

1 Strongly Disagree

2 Disagree

3 Neutral

4 Agree

5 Strongly Agree

Read the question and rate it with the following in front of mind:

'In my belief,
the answer to this question is clearly defined'.

There are two ways in which you can choose to interpret this statement;
1. how aware are you that the answer to the question is clearly defined
2. for more in-depth analysis you can choose to gather evidence and confirm the answer to the question. This obviously will take more time, most Self-Assessment users opt for the first way to interpret the question and dig deeper later on based on the outcome of the overall Self-Assessment.

A score of '1' would mean that the answer is not clear at all, where a '5' would mean the answer is crystal clear and defined. Leave emtpy when the question is not applicable or you don't want to answer it, you can skip it without affecting your score. Write your score in the space provided.

After you have responded to all the appropriate statements in each section, compute your average score for that section, using the formula provided, and round to the nearest tenth. Then transfer to the corresponding spoke in the SharePoint Online Office 365 Scorecard on the second next page of the Self-Assessment.

Your completed SharePoint Online Office 365 Scorecard will give you a clear presentation of which SharePoint Online Office 365 areas need attention.

SharePoint Online Office 365 Scorecard Example

Example of how the finalized Scorecard can look like:

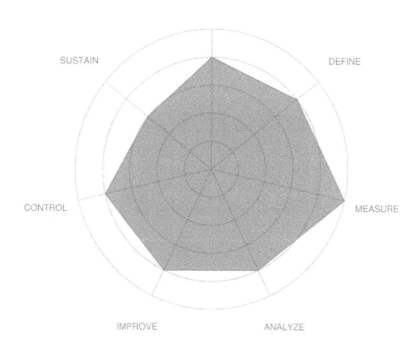

SharePoint Online Office 365 Scorecard

Your Scores:

BEGINNING OF THE SELF-ASSESSMENT:

CRITERION #1: RECOGNIZE

INTENT: Be aware of the need for change. Recognize that there is an unfavorable variation, problem or symptom.

In my belief, the answer to this question is clearly defined:

5 Strongly Agree

4 Agree

3 Neutral

2 Disagree

1 Strongly Disagree

1. Is the characterization of an event plausible and consistent with other events of this type?
<--- Score

2. What business need are you addressing?
<--- Score

3. Is there a specific event that you are required to audit?

<--- Score

4. Looking at this list of advantages and disadvantages, do you really need a mobile phone?
<--- Score

5. What needs to be done to bring new resources onto the team?
<--- Score

6. What type of project information do they need?
<--- Score

7. Do you need to provide management with visible progress throughout the project?
<--- Score

8. Are there any specific expectations or concerns about the SharePoint Online Office 365 team, SharePoint Online Office 365 itself?
<--- Score

9. How much productivity is lost cleaning up damage from compromises that could have been prevented?
<--- Score

10. How are the SharePoint Online Office 365's objectives aligned to the group's overall stakeholder strategy?
<--- Score

11. Does your organizations current IT staff have the appropriate skill set needed to support future organization technologies?

<--- Score

12. How are training requirements identified?
<--- Score

13. What SharePoint Online Office 365 capabilities do you need?
<--- Score

14. Do policies need to be exported to third-party security devices?
<--- Score

15. Do you need to provide customers with visible progress throughout the project?
<--- Score

16. Do you need separate levels for device-management permissions for IT roles and positions?
<--- Score

17. Who else hopes to benefit from it?
<--- Score

18. What resource levels do you need?
<--- Score

19. What extra resources will you need?
<--- Score

20. Have the staff that will be involved in the project been identified?
<--- Score

21. What are the expected benefits of SharePoint

Online Office 365 to the stakeholder?
<--- Score

22. What do you do if you need to do perform some logic that takes longer to execute?
<--- Score

23. How much are sponsors, customers, partners, stakeholders involved in SharePoint Online Office 365? In other words, what are the risks, if SharePoint Online Office 365 does not deliver successfully?
<--- Score

24. How does the system need to be operated?
<--- Score

25. Whom do you really need or want to serve?
<--- Score

26. What would happen if SharePoint Online Office 365 weren't done?
<--- Score

27. For your SharePoint Online Office 365 project, identify and describe the business environment, is there more than one layer to the business environment?
<--- Score

28. Do you need to use sharepoint designer?
<--- Score

29. Are you dealing with any of the same issues today as yesterday? What can you do about this?
<--- Score

30. How do you assess client needs for Office 365?
<--- Score

31. What structures need to be in place to deliver value?
<--- Score

32. Can your application prevent concurrent logins?
<--- Score

33. Will you need to control access to mobile apps?
<--- Score

34. What problems are you facing and how do you consider SharePoint Online Office 365 will circumvent those obstacles?
<--- Score

35. What do you need for identity delegation?
<--- Score

36. What is the problem and/or vulnerability?
<--- Score

37. To what extent would your organization benefit from being recognized as a award recipient?
<--- Score

38. How will issues and conflicts be addressed by your organization that may occur?
<--- Score

39. As a sponsor, customer or management, how important is it to meet goals, objectives?
<--- Score

40. Who is managing an event and what are some doing to respond to the incident?
<--- Score

41. One of your users needs to restore an early version of a file one deleted from SharePoint. Can you restore that version?
<--- Score

42. What does SharePoint Online Office 365 success mean to the stakeholders?
<--- Score

43. What situation(s) led to this SharePoint Online Office 365 Self Assessment?
<--- Score

44. What sorts of tools do you need to ensure scalability?
<--- Score

45. Does the system automatically index the events for reporting?
<--- Score

46. Are all functionalities already built up or do you need to customize Power BI and/or something else, before you can use them?
<--- Score

47. Will reports need to be shared or accessed remotely?
<--- Score

48. How do you remove a SharePoint site that is no

longer needed?
<--- Score

49. Is there a security concept for cloud use based on the security requirements identified?
<--- Score

50. Have all project stakeholders been identified?
<--- Score

51. Is it clear when the resources need to start on the project?
<--- Score

52. What are the stakeholder objectives to be achieved with SharePoint Online Office 365?
<--- Score

53. Your organization has a unique story, and like any great tale, it needs people to make it come alive. How do you get your employees excited about your vision?
<--- Score

54. Has an independent accountant identified separation of duties as a concern in the annual audit?
<--- Score

55. You need to determine, which accounts for automatic transactions are needed for the legal entity?
<--- Score

56. Revenue recognition - do the rules make sense?

<--- Score

57. What is the problem or issue?
<--- Score

58. How do you resolve issues with failure to provide deliverables on time, scope creep, personality conflicts, etc.?
<--- Score

59. Are all the interfaces identified?
<--- Score

60. Do users have rights to do everything they need to do in SharePoint?
<--- Score

61. What information do users need?
<--- Score

62. What do you need for hybrid?
<--- Score

63. Will organization computers need to be erased prior to the migration to Windows 10 and Office 365?
<--- Score

64. Do lookup codes (for things like order status, billing cycle, etc.) need to be cross-referenced?
<--- Score

65. What (ammunition, fuel, maintenance support) is needed by whom?
<--- Score

66. How are you going to measure success?
<--- Score

67. What is the trigger of project order handling?
<--- Score

68. What do you need to do if you want a SharePoint site?
<--- Score

69. Why do you need identity protection?
<--- Score

Add up total points for this section:
_ _ _ _ _ = Total points for this section

Divided by: _ _ _ _ _ _ (number of statements answered) = _ _ _ _ _ _
Average score for this section

Transfer your score to the SharePoint Online Office 365 Index at the beginning of the Self-Assessment.

CRITERION #2: DEFINE:

INTENT: Formulate the stakeholder problem. Define the problem, needs and objectives.

In my belief, the answer to this question is clearly defined:

5 Strongly Agree

4 Agree

3 Neutral

2 Disagree

1 Strongly Disagree

1. What constraints exist that might impact the team?
<--- Score

2. As an IT administrator, your biggest concerns are keeping your organization secure and meeting compliance requirements. and what are security and compliance for your organization?
<--- Score

3. Are there any changes in the definition of internal or external users and license requirements?

<--- Score

4. Is it a requirement to use SharePoint Online?

<--- Score

5. Has the SharePoint Online Office 365 work been fairly and/or equitably divided and delegated among team members who are qualified and capable to perform the work? Has everyone contributed?

<--- Score

6. In the case that the hardware specified is not providing the desired throughput or failover capabilities, who is responsible for providing the additional equipment?

<--- Score

7. Have all project stakeholders been defined?

<--- Score

8. Have the customer needs been translated into specific, measurable requirements? How?

<--- Score

9. Has the direction changed at all during the course of SharePoint Online Office 365? If so, when did it change and why?

<--- Score

10. How do you keep key subject matter experts in the loop?

<--- Score

11. What specifically is the problem? Where does it occur? When does it occur? What is its extent?
<--- Score

12. What regulatory or legal requirements exist that must be accounted for?
<--- Score

13. What are the Roles and Responsibilities for each team member and its leadership? Where is this documented?
<--- Score

14. Is the team formed and are team leaders (Coaches and Management Leads) assigned?
<--- Score

15. When is/was the SharePoint Online Office 365 start date?
<--- Score

16. How is the team tracking and documenting its work?
<--- Score

17. Which services are required and where will they be offered?
<--- Score

18. Is there a SharePoint Online Office 365 management charter, including stakeholder case, problem and goal statements, scope, milestones, roles and responsibilities, communication plan?
<--- Score

19. What is a good case study for the use of

Sharepoint as a tool for collaboration in an organization or network?
<--- Score

20. What key stakeholder process output measure(s) does SharePoint Online Office 365 leverage and how?
<--- Score

21. Is the SharePoint Online Office 365 scope manageable?
<--- Score

22. How does the SharePoint Online Office 365 manager ensure against scope creep?
<--- Score

23. How do you build the right business case?
<--- Score

24. What are the compelling stakeholder reasons for embarking on SharePoint Online Office 365?
<--- Score

25. How was the 'as is' process map developed, reviewed, verified and validated?
<--- Score

26. Have the roles and responsibilities - who does what - of the participants been defined?
<--- Score

27. How are labels and retention policies defined and configured?
<--- Score

28. Are there any constraints known that bear on the

ability to perform SharePoint Online Office 365 work? How is the team addressing them?
<--- Score

29. Is the team sponsored by a champion or stakeholder leader?
<--- Score

30. What tools do new resources require?
<--- Score

31. Are customers identified and high impact areas defined?
<--- Score

32. Are there any special error handling requirements?
<--- Score

33. What sources do you use to gather information for a SharePoint Online Office 365 study?
<--- Score

34. Online a requirement for corresponding Relationship KPIs to be available/possible?
<--- Score

35. Is there any additional SharePoint Online Office 365 definition of success?
<--- Score

36. Are there different segments of customers?
<--- Score

37. How will variation in the actual durations of each activity be dealt with to ensure that the expected

SharePoint Online Office 365 results are met?
<--- Score

38. Is SharePoint Online Office 365 currently on schedule according to the plan?
<--- Score

39. Has a project plan, Gantt chart, or similar been developed/completed?
<--- Score

40. Has a high-level 'as is' process map been completed, verified and validated?
<--- Score

41. If substitutes have been appointed, have they been briefed on the SharePoint Online Office 365 goals and received regular communications as to the progress to date?
<--- Score

42. Are improvement team members fully trained on SharePoint Online Office 365?
<--- Score

43. What are the boundaries of the scope? What is in bounds and what is not? What is the start point? What is the stop point?
<--- Score

44. Is SharePoint Online Office 365 linked to key stakeholder goals and objectives?
<--- Score

45. What are the rough order estimates on cost savings/opportunities that SharePoint Online Office

365 brings?

<--- Score

46. Is the work to date meeting requirements?

<--- Score

47. What is the nature of your requirements: seasonal, highly variable etc?

<--- Score

48. Is there any derived requirements concerning parts and functions?

<--- Score

49. Are there specific hardware requirements for Windows 10 and Office 365?

<--- Score

50. How often are the team meetings?

<--- Score

51. Does your organization have a clear business case for SharePoint. Why do you want it?

<--- Score

52. Is internet access required for office?

<--- Score

53. Are there any requirements to use the language interfaces (Java, C, COM, etc.) for integration?

<--- Score

54. Do all applications, projects or interfaces require the use of ?

<--- Score

55. Is it clearly defined in and to your organization what you do?
<--- Score

56. How will the SharePoint Online Office 365 team and the group measure complete success of SharePoint Online Office 365?
<--- Score

57. Is there a completed SIPOC representation, describing the Suppliers, Inputs, Process, Outputs, and Customers?
<--- Score

58. Is there regularly 100% attendance at the team meetings? If not, have appointed substitutes attended to preserve cross-functionality and full representation?
<--- Score

59. Will sharepoint be implemented on premise, hosted with a 3rd party provider, or in the cloud (sharepoint online). will a hybrid implementation be a requirement?
<--- Score

60. What customer feedback methods were used to solicit their input?
<--- Score

61. Have all basic functions of SharePoint Online Office 365 been defined?
<--- Score

62. Who is the resource delivering or receiving the

requirements?
<--- Score

63. Is a unified view of external content required?
<--- Score

64. Is data collected and displayed to better understand customer(s) critical needs and requirements.
<--- Score

65. Has a team charter been developed and communicated?
<--- Score

66. Has everyone on the team, including the team leaders, been properly trained?
<--- Score

67. Are stakeholder processes mapped?
<--- Score

68. What information do you gather?
<--- Score

69. What are the use cases for office 365?
<--- Score

70. Will team members perform SharePoint Online Office 365 work when assigned and in a timely fashion?
<--- Score

71. Will team members regularly document their SharePoint Online Office 365 work?
<--- Score

72. Has anyone else (internal or external to the group) attempted to solve this problem or a similar one before? If so, what knowledge can be leveraged from these previous efforts?
<--- Score

73. What are the core elements of the SharePoint Online Office 365 business case?
<--- Score

74. What are the dynamics of the communication plan?
<--- Score

75. Has/have the customer(s) been identified?
<--- Score

76. Is the current 'as is' process being followed? If not, what are the discrepancies?
<--- Score

77. What are the security requirements?
<--- Score

78. Are team charters developed?
<--- Score

79. Can you recommend additional Managed Security Services that are not currently included or considered in the scope of described services?
<--- Score

80. Does the budget contain all the resources required for successful completion of the project?
<--- Score

81. Is the improvement team aware of the different versions of a process: what they think it is vs. what it actually is vs. what it should be vs. what it could be?
<--- Score

82. What industry regulations are you required to meet?
<--- Score

83. Before you can perform a consolidation, which actions are required?
<--- Score

84. Can you define role-based access for individual users and specific resources?
<--- Score

85. Are different versions of process maps needed to account for the different types of inputs?
<--- Score

86. What would be the goal or target for a SharePoint Online Office 365's improvement team?
<--- Score

87. Is there any requirement of inbound/outbound fax?
<--- Score

88. Do the problem and goal statements meet the SMART criteria (specific, measurable, attainable, relevant, and time-bound)?
<--- Score

89. Does the team have regular meetings?

<--- Score

90. How are user-defined rules defined?
<--- Score

91. What are the reliability requirements?
<--- Score

92. Is a fully trained team formed, supported, and committed to work on the SharePoint Online Office 365 improvements?
<--- Score

93. Who are the SharePoint Online Office 365 improvement team members, including Management Leads and Coaches?
<--- Score

94. When is the estimated completion date?
<--- Score

95. What critical content must be communicated – who, what, when, where, and how?
<--- Score

96. Who is the resource delivering/receiving the requirements?
<--- Score

97. What level of integration is required with SharePoint?
<--- Score

98. What specific systems require integration?
<--- Score

99. Does your organization have any specific reports (defined format) that must exist at the time of go-live?

<--- Score

100. Are you constrained by a predefined schedule?

<--- Score

101. Has the improvement team collected the 'voice of the customer' (obtained feedback – qualitative and quantitative)?

<--- Score

102. When are meeting minutes sent out? Who is on the distribution list?

<--- Score

103. Is there a completed, verified, and validated high-level 'as is' (not 'should be' or 'could be') stakeholder process map?

<--- Score

104. Is full participation by members in regularly held team meetings guaranteed?

<--- Score

105. How did the SharePoint Online Office 365 manager receive input to the development of a SharePoint Online Office 365 improvement plan and the estimated completion dates/times of each activity?

<--- Score

106. Is there a critical path to deliver SharePoint Online Office 365 results?

<--- Score

107. Are customer(s) identified and segmented according to their different needs and requirements?
<--- Score

108. What are your office suite format requirements?
<--- Score

109. Is the team adequately staffed with the desired cross-functionality? If not, what additional resources are available to the team?
<--- Score

110. Is the team equipped with available and reliable resources?
<--- Score

Add up total points for this section:
_ _ _ _ _ = Total points for this section

Divided by: _ _ _ _ _ _ (number of statements answered) = _ _ _ _ _ _
Average score for this section

Transfer your score to the SharePoint Online Office 365 Index at the beginning of the Self-Assessment.

CRITERION #3: MEASURE:

INTENT: Gather the correct data. Measure the current performance and evolution of the situation.

In my belief, the answer to this question is clearly defined:

5 Strongly Agree

4 Agree

3 Neutral

2 Disagree

1 Strongly Disagree

1. Will sentiment analysis be added to relationship analytics, or will you focus on email and calendar counts as your insights?
<--- Score

2. How much time does your team spend investigating, prioritizing and confirming threats?
<--- Score

3. How large is the gap between current performance and the customer-specified (goal) performance?
<--- Score

4. What analytical skills are you interested in expanding or willing to expand to?
<--- Score

5. What are the key input variables? What are the key process variables? What are the key output variables?
<--- Score

6. What data was collected (past, present, future/ongoing)?
<--- Score

7. At what cost to privacy?
<--- Score

8. How do you prioritize your projects and assign resources?
<--- Score

9. How do you calculate the costs you might be missing?
<--- Score

10. What are the strategic priorities for this year?
<--- Score

11. How will the cost of Office 365 be charged (annually, monthly)?
<--- Score

12. Is key measure data collection planned and executed, process variation displayed and

communicated and performance baselined?
<--- Score

13. If you have tens of thousands of external users will SharePoint online performance be impacted?
<--- Score

14. Is long term and short term variability accounted for?
<--- Score

15. How often do you review your organizational chart?
<--- Score

16. Are process variation components displayed/ communicated using suitable charts, graphs, plots?
<--- Score

17. Is there a Performance Baseline?
<--- Score

18. Have you found any 'ground fruit' or 'low-hanging fruit' for immediate remedies to the gap in performance?
<--- Score

19. How can you manage cost down?
<--- Score

20. Was a SharePoint Online Office 365 charter developed?
<--- Score

21. How should you prioritize your projects and assign resources?

<--- Score

22. What is given up in order to save (opportunity cost of saving)?

<--- Score

23. How much does it cost and how does it provide value for money?

<--- Score

24. Is Process Variation Displayed/Communicated?

<--- Score

25. Are you aware of what could cause a problem?

<--- Score

26. Are documents impacted by the GRC solution stored exclusively in SharePoint?

<--- Score

27. Are you confident that you have identified all priority business data assets and location?

<--- Score

28. What particular quality tools did the team find helpful in establishing measurements?

<--- Score

29. What does it costs to operate and maintain the IT Investment?

<--- Score

30. How to cause the change?

<--- Score

31. What system changes would cause the

integrity check on your operating system drive to fail?

<--- Score

32. What effect should the system cause?

<--- Score

33. Who participated in the data collection for measurements?

<--- Score

34. Is a solid data collection plan established that includes measurement systems analysis?

<--- Score

35. Was a data collection plan established?

<--- Score

36. Is data collection planned and executed?

<--- Score

37. Has a cost benefit analysis been performed?

<--- Score

38. Who (which unit) has priority of support?

<--- Score

39. How can you take advantage of low cost, highly available cloud services?

<--- Score

40. Is there industry focus being put on the development of the sales app?

<--- Score

41. Are high impact defects defined and identified in

the stakeholder process?

<--- Score

42. Can you measure the return on analysis?

<--- Score

43. What could cause delays in the schedule?

<--- Score

44. How do you prioritize ?

<--- Score

45. Are key measures identified and agreed upon?

<--- Score

46. When is Root Cause Analysis Required?

<--- Score

47. What are predictive SharePoint Online Office 365 analytics?

<--- Score

48. Is data collected on key measures that were identified?

<--- Score

49. What has the team done to assure the stability and accuracy of the measurement process?

<--- Score

50. What key measures identified indicate the performance of the stakeholder process?

<--- Score

51. What do you measure and why?

<--- Score

52. What are the agreed upon definitions of the high impact areas, defect(s), unit(s), and opportunities that will figure into the process capability metrics?
<--- Score

53. Will SharePoint Online Office 365 have an impact on current business continuity, disaster recovery processes and/or infrastructure?
<--- Score

54. Does consideration of cost seem reasonable?
<--- Score

55. What savings/avoided costs are estimated with re-engineering?
<--- Score

56. What causes mismanagement?
<--- Score

57. How do you stay flexible and focused to recognize larger SharePoint Online Office 365 results?
<--- Score

58. What best practices are recommended to ensure no impact to the Production system?
<--- Score

59. What charts has the team used to display the components of variation in the process?
<--- Score

60. How do you use Log Analytics?
<--- Score

61. Has the impact of cost overruns been analyzed?

<--- Score

62. How does the cloud impact and interface with the goals of IT Optimization?

<--- Score

63. What will the cost for Office 365 be to departments?

<--- Score

64. Do staff have the necessary skills to collect, analyze, and report data?

<--- Score

65. What harm might be caused?

<--- Score

66. Security metrics: what can you measure?

<--- Score

67. Has the impact of late delivery been analyzed?

<--- Score

68. What impact did this activity have on perception of banking needs and decision making?

<--- Score

69. How do you guarantee that each user will have his or her own dedicated resources and cannot impact each other?

<--- Score

Add up total points for this section:

_____ = Total points for this section

Divided by: _____ (number of statements answered) = _____ Average score for this section

Transfer your score to the SharePoint Online Office 365 Index at the beginning of the Self-Assessment.

CRITERION #4: ANALYZE:

INTENT: Analyze causes, assumptions and hypotheses.

In my belief, the answer to this question is clearly defined:

5 Strongly Agree

4 Agree

3 Neutral

2 Disagree

1 Strongly Disagree

1. Strategies for reporting in Finance and Operations: Should you build a data warehouse?
<--- Score

2. Are gaps between current performance and the goal performance identified?
<--- Score

3. What migration tools do you provide to move local data to the cloud, if any?

<--- Score

4. What data and data types do you need?
<--- Score

5. Is the decision to perform your organizations own data backups justified and documented?
<--- Score

6. Are your documents stored in OneDrive also available offline?
<--- Score

7. What were the crucial 'moments of truth' on the process map?
<--- Score

8. How rigorous of a backup and recovery process will you require?
<--- Score

9. What data can you store/share on OneDrive/SharePoint/Teams?
<--- Score

10. Is the gap/opportunity displayed and communicated in financial terms?
<--- Score

11. Did any value-added analysis or 'lean thinking' take place to identify some of the gaps shown on the 'as is' process map?
<--- Score

12. How do you prevent data leakage?
<--- Score

13. Were any designed experiments used to generate additional insight into the data analysis?
<--- Score

14. What conclusions were drawn from the team's data collection and analysis? How did the team reach these conclusions?
<--- Score

15. What is the process to create a site?
<--- Score

16. What is your organizations process for regular review of its financial management policies?
<--- Score

17. Why object-process methodology?
<--- Score

18. Do other systems share or have access to data/ information in this system?
<--- Score

19. What are the sources and types of the data/ information in the system?
<--- Score

20. Is the performance gap determined?
<--- Score

21. Word processing applications: one or several?
<--- Score

22. Does your application show user permissions for files in Microsoft OneDrive?

<--- Score

23. How are the new Business Process Flows exposed on the client side?
<--- Score

24. Who will help with the database conversions when new versions are pushed out?
<--- Score

25. What are the technology replacement opportunities?
<--- Score

26. How does office 365 affect data retention practices?
<--- Score

27. What level of technical ability is required to create new workflow processes, modify existing workflow processes?
<--- Score

28. What did the team gain from developing a sub-process map?
<--- Score

29. What resources go in to get desired output?
<--- Score

30. How sensitive is the data you are interested in using and how will you control and restrict access?
<--- Score

31. What is the requirement for bringing in your existing data?

<--- Score

32. Who qualifies to gain access to data?
<--- Score

33. How do you improve business processes and how do you deliver on that?
<--- Score

34. What is the difference between SharePoint Online and OneDrive for Business?
<--- Score

35. Does your application show data business owners?
<--- Score

36. What process does your organization use to minimize financial risks of investments?
<--- Score

37. What is the difference between OneDrive for Business and SharePoint Online?
<--- Score

38. How was the detailed process map generated, verified, and validated?
<--- Score

39. Have scope changes followed the documented scope/change management approval process?
<--- Score

40. Is data and process analysis, root cause analysis and quantifying the gap/opportunity in place?
<--- Score

41. Does your organization have a preferred payment processing system that will be used with this new system?
<--- Score

42. What is identity-driven security?
<--- Score

43. What reconciliations will be used for each data type?
<--- Score

44. What is the process for making changes to the personnel policies?
<--- Score

45. Are data management policies, procedures, and business rules adequately being addressed?
<--- Score

46. Are current it service delivery and processes adequate to meet short and long term department needs?
<--- Score

47. Are the contractual agreements appropriate in type, scope and level of detail for the protection requirements of the data and the applications connected with the cloud service usage?
<--- Score

48. How can you use the renewal process to ensure that your organization is covered, including any light users that do not need the full suite?
<--- Score

49. Simply delivering process information to the right users is not enough: how can you ensure that the process information is meaningful, accurate and up-to-date?
<--- Score

50. What does the data say about the performance of the stakeholder process?
<--- Score

51. What is in the future for SharePoint, Office 365, and OneDrive for Business?
<--- Score

52. How can you secure your enterprise data in Office 365?
<--- Score

53. You keep record of data and store them in cloud services; for example Google Suite. There are data protection tools provided and security rules can be set. But who has the responsibility for securing them - us or Google?
<--- Score

54. What devices are accessing data stored in SharePoint Online and where are the already stated devices accessing from?
<--- Score

55. If your organization used electronic payments what are the approval and review processes?
<--- Score

56. What were the financial benefits resulting from

any 'ground fruit or low-hanging fruit' (quick fixes)?
<--- Score

57. What are the best opportunities for value improvement?
<--- Score

58. How does database as a service make sense for an enterprise like your organization?
<--- Score

59. Are current systems consistent with industry best practices for seamless integration of workflow and data?
<--- Score

60. Will the licensing database and software system be required to integrate with any external systems?
<--- Score

61. Is sensitive data being shared with third parties outside your organization?
<--- Score

62. How do you search for data across multiple databases?
<--- Score

63. Is it possible to implement interactive data exploration methods?
<--- Score

64. What is the difference between Enterprise Information Management and Data Warehousing?
<--- Score

65. To what extent would you enable the end user to manipulate the data, if at all?
<--- Score

66. Did any additional data need to be collected?
<--- Score

67. How can you ensure you comply with internal and external data protection requirements?
<--- Score

68. What is needed to convert a current Business Process Flow to the new ones?
<--- Score

69. Is the required SharePoint Online Office 365 data gathered?
<--- Score

70. Does the GDPR apply to your data?
<--- Score

71. Collected, for example, where does the data need to go when you are finished with it?
<--- Score

72. Is the SharePoint Online Office 365 process severely broken such that a re-design is necessary?
<--- Score

73. What resources go in to get desired output after changes?
<--- Score

74. Is data classification really needed?

<--- Score

75. What other jobs or tasks affect the performance of the steps in the SharePoint Online Office 365 process?
<--- Score

76. Is there a file size limit for searching data?
<--- Score

77. How do you customize the business processes for your business?
<--- Score

78. What is the recovery process like?
<--- Score

79. Do organizational changes follow a documented change management approval process?
<--- Score

80. What is your organizations process for the development of its financial management policies?
<--- Score

81. What quality tools were used to get through the analyze phase?
<--- Score

82. How do you open file on shared drive?
<--- Score

83. Required processing time for each transaction?
<--- Score

84. How do you apply mobile app management policies to B2B users accessing organization data?
<--- Score

85. Where is the Office 365 Groups data stored?
<--- Score

86. What do you do if data is lost and/or your infrastructure is corrupted?
<--- Score

87. How has the SharePoint Online Office 365 data been gathered?
<--- Score

88. Are your paper-based processes eating your profits?
<--- Score

89. How will your organizations approach to data conversion provide data integrity?
<--- Score

90. Do your applications include DLP (Data Loss Protection) capabilities?
<--- Score

91. Were there any improvement opportunities identified from the process analysis?
<--- Score

92. Volume of messages or transactions that need to be processed per hour?
<--- Score

93. What APIs should you use for accessing the

data you need?
<--- Score

94. Was a detailed process map created to amplify critical steps of the 'as is' stakeholder process?
<--- Score

95. What areas of your organization need a baseline level of data protection?
<--- Score

96. Additional business needs in a complex hybrid environment, is data classification really needed?
<--- Score

97. Who will have access to the data/information in the system (internal and external parties)?
<--- Score

98. How can you build a secure warehouse from the data sources?
<--- Score

99. How can you determine when to use OneDrive for Business, SharePoint, and eDMRM?
<--- Score

100. Is the contractor responsible for implementing a backup strategy to minimize loss of data?
<--- Score

101. What level of latency are you comfortable with in accessing the data?
<--- Score

102. What tools were used to narrow the list of possible causes?

<--- Score

103. How often is the data backed up?

<--- Score

104. Were Pareto charts (or similar) used to portray the 'heavy hitters' (or key sources of variation)?

<--- Score

105. What are the target business processes your organization would like to improve with this initial project?

<--- Score

106. What qualifications and skills do you need?

<--- Score

107. What tools were used to generate the list of possible causes?

<--- Score

108. Was a cause-and-effect diagram used to explore the different types of causes (or sources of variation)?

<--- Score

109. Can you do complex searches with field qualifiers, bracketing/nesting of search terms along with Boolean operators such as AND, OR, NOT, NEAR?

<--- Score

110. How do you prevent data leakage from your mobile apps?

<--- Score

111. Risk of data exfiltration - Do you know what your users are sharing?

<--- Score

112. What is the cost of poor quality as supported by the team's analysis?

<--- Score

113. Have any additional benefits been identified that will result from closing all or most of the gaps?

<--- Score

114. How much do you know about your data backup process?

<--- Score

115. The problem of personal data in cloud computing: what information is regulated?

<--- Score

116. Do the shared drives you work with follow a common directory naming structure?

<--- Score

117. How will data be protected on devices at rest and in transit?

<--- Score

118. What is the difference between OneDrive for Business and SharePoint team sites?

<--- Score

119. What are the needs for the process of system knowledge capture and reuse?

<--- Score

120. Identify an operational issue in your organization, for example, could a particular task be done more quickly or more efficiently by SharePoint Online Office 365?
<--- Score

121. What criteria and transformations will be performed during the conversion process?
<--- Score

122. You need to prevent the sales order from being processed. What should you do?
<--- Score

123. Which SharePoint Online Office 365 data should be retained?
<--- Score

124. Have the problem and goal statements been updated to reflect the additional knowledge gained from the analyze phase?
<--- Score

125. Is there any script to upload data?
<--- Score

126. How much time does it take for IT to perform e-discovery and data export?
<--- Score

127. Do you, as a leader, bounce back quickly from setbacks?
<--- Score

128. What types of information can you store on

OneDrive for business and SharePoint online?
<--- Score

129. Sensitivity of the data in the system or the system functionality?
<--- Score

130. Do you have the required search criteria available to find logs quickly?
<--- Score

131. Does your application search files in cloud storage Microsoft OneDrive?
<--- Score

132. What are the revised rough estimates of the financial savings/opportunity for SharePoint Online Office 365 improvements?
<--- Score

Add up total points for this section:
_ _ _ _ _ = Total points for this section

Divided by: _ _ _ _ _ _ (number of statements answered) = _ _ _ _ _ _
Average score for this section

Transfer your score to the SharePoint Online Office 365 Index at the beginning of the Self-Assessment.

CRITERION #5: IMPROVE:

INTENT: Develop a practical solution.
Innovate, establish and test the
solution and to measure the results.

In my belief, the answer to this
question is clearly defined:

5 Strongly Agree

4 Agree

3 Neutral

2 Disagree

1 Strongly Disagree

1. What lessons, if any, from a pilot were incorporated into the design of the full-scale solution?
<--- Score

2. Is pilot data collected and analyzed?
<--- Score

3. What tools were used to tap into the creativity and encourage 'outside the box' thinking?

<--- Score

4. How did the team generate the list of possible solutions?
<--- Score

5. What tools were most useful during the improve phase?
<--- Score

6. Is there a cost/benefit analysis of optimal solution(s)?
<--- Score

7. Where will your email and documents be stored once you are using Office 365?
<--- Score

8. Is the optimal solution selected based on testing and analysis?
<--- Score

9. What security and compliance risks are introduced when well-intentioned users resort to personal email to get work done?
<--- Score

10. What SharePoint skills do you currently have in house in terms of SharePoint Administration, Maintenance, Content Owner/Authorship, and Development?
<--- Score

11. What is the team's contingency plan for potential problems occurring in implementation?
<--- Score

12. How scalable is your SharePoint Online Office 365 solution?

<--- Score

13. Will you use SharePoint online, custom, third party or SharePoint server based solutions?

<--- Score

14. Were any criteria developed to assist the team in testing and evaluating potential solutions?

<--- Score

15. What is the magnitude of the improvements?

<--- Score

16. Is the implementation plan designed?

<--- Score

17. To what extent do you believe the Framework has helped reduce your cybersecurity risk?

<--- Score

18. Which users will have the right to the premium and expensive solution, who will have to settle for the basic version?

<--- Score

19. Does your organization currently have a preferred document management system of choice?

<--- Score

20. Technical team who will lead the design and development of the integration solution?

<--- Score

21. What tools were used to evaluate the potential solutions?

<--- Score

22. What result is desired?

<--- Score

23. What error proofing will be done to address some of the discrepancies observed in the 'as is' process?

<--- Score

24. What is the implementation plan?

<--- Score

25. Are new and improved process ('should be') maps developed?

<--- Score

26. How does the Board of Directors become aware of potential risks facing your organization?

<--- Score

27. How can microsoft help you understand your current security posture and get recommendations on how to improve it?

<--- Score

28. What is the risk?

<--- Score

29. Does your organization need a central solution to manage On-Premise and cloud services at the same time?

<--- Score

30. Did you see any relationship between the degree of risk and the level of return you expected?
<--- Score

31. Are the risks fully understood, reasonable and manageable?
<--- Score

32. What do you need to do to understand your organization of business and your work?
<--- Score

33. Is there a small-scale pilot for proposed improvement(s)? What conclusions were drawn from the outcomes of a pilot?
<--- Score

34. Would you develop a SharePoint Online Office 365 Communication Strategy?
<--- Score

35. How could the vendor offer solutions that you would value with or without a breach?
<--- Score

36. Do you have additional Improvement Requests?
<--- Score

37. What key decisions were made?
<--- Score

38. Are the most efficient solutions problem-specific?
<--- Score

39. What are the areas in which your organization would like to improve?
<--- Score

40. Describe the design of the pilot and what tests were conducted, if any?
<--- Score

41. Published intranet sites are rarely the only SharePoint solution deployed within an organization. How will you integrate other solutions with your published intranet?
<--- Score

42. Is your organization looking for Microsoft SharePoint to be a read only consumption model, or a creation model for documents as well?
<--- Score

43. Was a pilot designed for the proposed solution(s)?
<--- Score

44. What are the SharePoint Online Office 365 security risks?
<--- Score

45. Are you assessing SharePoint Online Office 365 and risk?
<--- Score

46. Is any SharePoint Online Office 365 documentation required?
<--- Score

47. Are the best solutions selected?
<--- Score

48. What is SharePoint Online Office 365's impact on utilizing the best solution(s)?
<--- Score

49. What are the security risks presented by migration to Microsoft?
<--- Score

50. How well does the solution provide enterprise capabilities for security and authentication?
<--- Score

51. Would the system be better as a result?
<--- Score

52. Is the SharePoint Online Office 365 solution sustainable?
<--- Score

53. Is risk periodically assessed?
<--- Score

54. Is a solution implementation plan established, including schedule/work breakdown structure, resources, risk management plan, cost/budget, and control plan?
<--- Score

55. Can you use Office 365 ProPlus with a partner-hosted solution?
<--- Score

56. What does the 'should be' process map/design look like?
<--- Score

57. What communications are necessary to support the implementation of the solution?
<--- Score

58. Are improved process ('should be') maps modified based on pilot data and analysis?
<--- Score

59. What resources are required for the improvement efforts?
<--- Score

60. Risk Identification: What are the possible risk events your organization faces in relation to SharePoint Online Office 365?
<--- Score

61. Are possible solutions generated and tested?
<--- Score

62. Need more information on how to evaluate your accounting and operations solutions?
<--- Score

63. Can the cisco sd-wan solution provide optimization for IaaS and SaaS platforms like aws, microsoft azure and office 365, google, salesforce. com, cisco webex, etc?
<--- Score

64. Are risk triggers captured?
<--- Score

65. How will you know that a change is an improvement?

<--- Score

66. Privileged account actions, are users with sensitive information at risk?

<--- Score

67. How do you implement a vulnerability assessment solution?

<--- Score

68. Is the master contractor providing timesheets or other appropriate documentation to support invoices?

<--- Score

69. How do you embrace the benefits of cloud-based email and productivity solutions without compromising security or adding risk?

<--- Score

70. What records are created to document the beginning and ending times of employees actual workshifts?

<--- Score

71. What are typical and effective solutions used by other organizations of your size?

<--- Score

72. What do you want to document in the model?

<--- Score

73. Are there any constraints (technical, political, cultural, or otherwise) that would inhibit certain solutions?

<--- Score

74. Does your organization intend to use Microsoft SharePoint web content management and publishing features outside of the EDM solution?
<--- Score

75. What are the security risks to email/file sharing?
<--- Score

76. How will the team or the process owner(s) monitor the implementation plan to see that it is working as intended?
<--- Score

77. If there are multiple good options, how to evaluate the pros and cons for a particular workload?
<--- Score

78. What can you do to improve?
<--- Score

79. How does the solution remove the key sources of issues discovered in the analyze phase?
<--- Score

80. Is a contingency plan established?
<--- Score

81. Do you combine technical expertise with business knowledge and SharePoint Online Office 365 Key topics include lifecycles, development approaches, requirements and how to make a business case?
<--- Score

82. What were the underlying assumptions on the cost-benefit analysis?

<--- Score

83. What attendant changes will need to be made to ensure that the solution is successful?

<--- Score

84. How does your organization use evaluation in developing, reviewing and/or revising security programs?

<--- Score

85. Are there any requirements around storage design for your virtualized SharePoint solution?

<--- Score

86. Does your organization use Microsoft SharePoint Server (MOSS) for IT collaboration needs around the EDM solution?

<--- Score

87. Is the role of SharePoint primarily to be a document repository with some method of providing a link to the applicable documents from aware?

<--- Score

88. How will the group know that the solution worked?

<--- Score

Add up total points for this section:

_ _ _ _ _ = Total points for this section

Divided by: _ _ _ _ _ _ (number of

statements answered) = _ _ _ _ _ _
Average score for this section

Transfer your score to the SharePoint
Online Office 365 Index at the
beginning of the Self-Assessment.

CRITERION #6: CONTROL:

INTENT: Implement the practical solution. Maintain the performance and correct possible complications.

In my belief, the answer to this question is clearly defined:

5 Strongly Agree

4 Agree

3 Neutral

2 Disagree

1 Strongly Disagree

1. Will your system have the capability to identify, locate, and monitor individuals or groups of people?
<--- Score

2. How does securing executive sponsorship contribute to an enterprise resource plannings success?
<--- Score

3. How will the process owner and team be able to hold the gains?
<--- Score

4. Does the system require a System Test Plan?
<--- Score

5. What quality tools were useful in the control phase?
<--- Score

6. Do you have a plan for managing your sprawl?
<--- Score

7. Do the SharePoint Online Office 365 decisions you make today help people and the planet tomorrow?
<--- Score

8. What other systems, operations, processes, and infrastructures (hiring practices, staffing, training, incentives/rewards, metrics/dashboards/scorecards, etc.) need updates, additions, changes, or deletions in order to facilitate knowledge transfer and improvements?
<--- Score

9. Are suggested corrective/restorative actions indicated on the response plan for known causes to problems that might surface?
<--- Score

10. How do senior leaders actions reflect a commitment to the organizations SharePoint Online Office 365 values?
<--- Score

11. Which applications are you planning to host in the cloud?

<--- Score

12. Is it possible to scale the processing of events to several machines?

<--- Score

13. How does getting help from outside experts contribute to your enterprises resource planning success?

<--- Score

14. What level of monitoring is provided by the Contractor?

<--- Score

15. Will your organization be managing the SharePoint Active Directory, and is there a service level agreement or standard for how long it takes to complete a service request?

<--- Score

16. Does job training on the documented procedures need to be part of the process team's education and training?

<--- Score

17. How often do you anticipate needing to scale your solution up or down?

<--- Score

18. Are there any plans for the tracking to be available for emails created in Outlook?

<--- Score

19. Are the financial auditors confident in ability to assess risks associated with enterprise resource planning systems?
<--- Score

20. Is there a transfer of ownership and knowledge to process owner and process team tasked with the responsibilities.
<--- Score

21. Do you have privacy controls for communications?
<--- Score

22. Do have any concerns or recommendations regarding how to scale Managed Security Services to organizations of the size and complexity of your organization?
<--- Score

23. Is the SharePoint Online Office 365 test/ monitoring cost justified?
<--- Score

24. Have you coordinated your planning with the community or state emergency operation center?
<--- Score

25. How will the process owner verify improvement in present and future sigma levels, process capabilities?
<--- Score

26. How can enterprise resource planning facilitate organizational transformation?
<--- Score

27. Does the composition of the staff reflect the demographics of the community?

<--- Score

28. Is a response plan established and deployed?

<--- Score

29. Does the SharePoint Online Office 365 performance meet the customer's requirements?

<--- Score

30. What regulations and standards does your solution need to meet?

<--- Score

31. Are enterprise resource planning and business process reengineering right for you?

<--- Score

32. Is new knowledge gained imbedded in the response plan?

<--- Score

33. Does the system differentiate standard storage from archival of old events?

<--- Score

34. Does the response plan contain a definite closed loop continual improvement scheme (e.g., plan-do-check-act)?

<--- Score

35. How do you plan to deploy the clients?

<--- Score

36. Are documented procedures clear and easy to

follow for the operators?

<--- Score

37. How will report readings be checked to effectively monitor performance?

<--- Score

38. Are your organizations financial auditors confident in ability to assess risks associated with enterprise resource planning systems?

<--- Score

39. Is knowledge gained on process shared and institutionalized?

<--- Score

40. Is there a standardized process?

<--- Score

41. Is there a documented and implemented monitoring plan?

<--- Score

42. Do testing plans align with industry standards and build confidence in the integrity of the test process?

<--- Score

43. Will any special training be provided for results interpretation?

<--- Score

44. Does enterprise resource planning systems add productivity to a business enterprise?

<--- Score

45. Which steps should be a part of your incident response plan?

<--- Score

46. Where do you plan on hosting your data, locally or in the cloud?

<--- Score

47. Will marketing be included in customer engagement plan?

<--- Score

48. Has the improved process and its steps been standardized?

<--- Score

49. Are operating procedures consistent?

<--- Score

50. What should the next improvement project be that is related to SharePoint Online Office 365?

<--- Score

51. How much do you need to plan ahead and design ahead during this project for future versions?

<--- Score

52. Is there documentation that will support the successful operation of the improvement?

<--- Score

53. Does the quality management plan reflect the quality assurance activities being conducted?

<--- Score

54. What are customers monitoring?
<--- Score

55. Are there documented procedures?
<--- Score

56. What key inputs and outputs are being measured on an ongoing basis?
<--- Score

57. How do you control and release a new range of products?
<--- Score

58. Can you provide a preliminary plan and timeline on how the existing services could be migrated to a new vendor without interrupting services?
<--- Score

59. What other areas of the group might benefit from the SharePoint Online Office 365 team's improvements, knowledge, and learning?
<--- Score

60. What activities should you monitor in Office 365?
<--- Score

61. What can you control?
<--- Score

62. Is reporting being used or needed?
<--- Score

63. Will the project add-in work with project

standard, or is professional mandatory?
<--- Score

64. Who is the SharePoint Online Office 365 process owner?
<--- Score

65. How will input, process, and output variables be checked to detect for sub-optimal conditions?
<--- Score

66. Is there a recommended audit plan for routine surveillance inspections of SharePoint Online Office 365's gains?
<--- Score

67. What is the impact of enterprise resource planning on supporting supply chain management?
<--- Score

68. What is the control/monitoring plan?
<--- Score

69. Do enterprise resource planning systems add productivity to a business enterprise?
<--- Score

70. Do you have what it takes to survive an unplanned interruption?
<--- Score

71. Role based access control. what is it in your organization?
<--- Score

72. Is the plan to use SharePoint for collaboration (WIP) content and controlled records?

<--- Score

73. How do you control access to mobile apps?

<--- Score

74. Will a SaaS model imply a standardized solution?

<--- Score

75. Will it become your corporate standard for user file sharing?

<--- Score

76. Where do you find detailed information about functionality licensed via Applications, Plans, and Team Members subscriptions?

<--- Score

77. How might the group capture best practices and lessons learned so as to leverage improvements?

<--- Score

78. What tools do you use to monitor Office 365?

<--- Score

79. Will it become your corporate standard for user file storage and sharing?

<--- Score

80. As part of a governance plan, did you determine who does what? For example, who creates sites, who controls keywords in Search, or who manages the metadata and ensures that the metadata is applied correctly?

<--- Score

81. Are the planned controls in place?
<--- Score

82. How will new or emerging customer needs/
requirements be checked/communicated to orient
the process toward meeting the new specifications
and continually reducing variation?
<--- Score

83. How will the day-to-day responsibilities for
monitoring and continual improvement be
transferred from the improvement team to the
process owner?
<--- Score

**84. Are financial auditors overconfident in ability
to assess risks associated with enterprise resource
planning systems?**
<--- Score

**85. How do you control security roles across the
different apps?**
<--- Score

86. Is a response plan in place for when the input,
process, or output measures indicate an 'out-of-
control' condition?
<--- Score

87. Does a troubleshooting guide exist or is it needed?
<--- Score

88. Are new process steps, standards, and
documentation ingrained into normal operations?

<--- Score

89. What are the critical parameters to watch?
<--- Score

90. Are there plans to leverage e-commerce opportunities via a mobile app?
<--- Score

91. Is the overall move to the cloud environment reflecting what was expected?
<--- Score

92. Is there a control plan in place for sustaining improvements (short and long-term)?
<--- Score

93. Have new or revised work instructions resulted?
<--- Score

94. What is the recommended frequency of auditing?
<--- Score

Add up total points for this section:
_ _ _ _ _ = Total points for this section

Divided by: _ _ _ _ _ _ (number of statements answered) = _ _ _ _ _ _
Average score for this section

Transfer your score to the SharePoint Online Office 365 Index at the beginning of the Self-Assessment.

CRITERION #7: SUSTAIN:

INTENT: Retain the benefits.

In my belief, the answer to this question is clearly defined:

5 Strongly Agree

4 Agree

3 Neutral

2 Disagree

1 Strongly Disagree

1. Does your application show user permissions for files in SharePoint Online?
<--- Score

2. Is this a single infection that went no further than the endpoint?
<--- Score

3. What types of activities will resonate with your leadership and your employees?
<--- Score

4. When should you use Microsoft Teams and Office 365 Groups?

<--- Score

5. How long will it take?

<--- Score

6. What is your secure environment?

<--- Score

7. How well does the Vendor Project Manager, Account Manager and Key Personnel present information and address questions?

<--- Score

8. What is the exit strategy to leave O365?

<--- Score

9. How many moss front ends does your organization currently have?

<--- Score

10. Can two internal approvals be reduced to one?

<--- Score

11. How dependent should you/will you be on Microsoft technologies (e.g., Active Directory) for your security management?

<--- Score

12. Is there an option to participate only in the email portion of Office 365?

<--- Score

13. When do you use which varying types of

communication?

<--- Score

14. How is a purchase order created?

<--- Score

15. Is a current maintenance agreement in place for all of the technologies to be implemented?

<--- Score

16. What degree of vetting is appropriate to check payment information supplied by the customer?

<--- Score

17. Does the system support integration with cloud storage services such as Amazon S3?

<--- Score

18. Lack of visibility into existing malware - Do you have retrospective security if a file becomes malicious after the initial point of inspection?

<--- Score

19. Is teams call recording enabled?

<--- Score

20. For a staff augmentation project, what is the extent of the vendors project managers engagement?

<--- Score

21. Are there benefits to your organization to pursue a single procurement for Microsoft licenses rather than separate purchases under separate EAs?

<--- Score

22. What types of hybrid are available?
<--- Score

23. If your organization does not have the staff or funding to meet increasing demand for IT services, how will IT leadership fulfill the requests?
<--- Score

24. What is it that alerts you to the fact that this is a scam, and not a genuine offer?
<--- Score

25. What is application access and single sign-on with Azure Active Directory in your organization?
<--- Score

26. How do you account for ideas to each other?
<--- Score

27. What is the vendor support and licensing model?
<--- Score

28. Does office 365 come with an email archive (currently known as enterprise vault)?
<--- Score

29. How do topologies work in practice?
<--- Score

30. Do you have an incident response workflow in place to remediate any situation?
<--- Score

31. What are two features of Relationship Insights

that can be used to accomplish this?
<--- Score

32. Does this system use social media channels?
<--- Score

33. Are your family and you safe?
<--- Score

34. What are the infrastructure constraints?
<--- Score

35. What is the criticality if your end users can not perform tasks?
<--- Score

36. How do you ensure a great experience for your clients?
<--- Score

37. How will migrating to Office 365 change things for me?
<--- Score

38. How do you target content to specific audiences?
<--- Score

39. What about the archiving options available from Microsoft?
<--- Score

40. How does licensing work in a SharePoint hybrid cloud?
<--- Score

41. If a device is selectively wiped, should it automatically be unenrolled from management?
<--- Score

42. How do you know if SharePoint Online is right for your organization?
<--- Score

43. How do you propose your organization request Key Management services?
<--- Score

44. What do you do for staff who have mailboxes both on-premises and in Office 365?
<--- Score

45. Are any third party training resources proposed?
<--- Score

46. What is the main purpose/function of the systems?
<--- Score

47. What services can integrate?
<--- Score

48. Are you meeting the objectives of the client?
<--- Score

49. How will team members knowledge management use rights change?
<--- Score

50. Where will the software and adapters be installed?

<--- Score

51. How can governance be used to achieve the wide range of performance expectations?
<--- Score

52. Do you have a virtual desktop environment for staff to use?
<--- Score

53. What were the rights and responsibilities of both the consumer and the insurance organization?
<--- Score

54. Do you have access to all the content?
<--- Score

55. Do you currently use Modern SharePoint sites or pages?
<--- Score

56. Are you providing the right level of credit to the right customers?
<--- Score

57. Does the sharepoint portal use an existing single sign-on system like ldap or active directory?
<--- Score

58. What options do you offer customers that do not want to go the cloud?
<--- Score

59. For whom is the system built?
<--- Score

60. Can you enable single-sign-on with other cloud based SaaS services?
<--- Score

61. What are the most common security concerns voiced by your customers?
<--- Score

62. How can corresponding be reconciled?
<--- Score

63. Are there existing infrastructures that are serving as a barrier?
<--- Score

64. How do you recover sooner?
<--- Score

65. Or outlook block certain file types?
<--- Score

66. What are the major system design alternatives?
<--- Score

67. How has communication evolved in your organization?
<--- Score

68. Who does your organization contact if application testing discovers incompatibility with Windows 10 or Office 365 in a mission critical application?
<--- Score

69. What are your Service Level Agreements

(SLAs)?
<--- Score

70. What are the versions of the applications involved?
<--- Score

71. How do you use tools, such as SharePoint, Wikis or other collaborative work spaces?
<--- Score

72. How can your organization demonstrate appropriate empathy?
<--- Score

73. How often are message logs indexed?
<--- Score

74. What is the minimum time in which temporary systems may be expected to become available?
<--- Score

75. Why now?
<--- Score

76. How will you manage existing Teams and create new ones?
<--- Score

77. Does the system support a pre-configured set of rules and actions?
<--- Score

78. Do you use Microsoft Power BI or other business intelligence (BI) tools?
<--- Score

79. What should be accomplished?

<--- Score

80. How does your organization approach the SharePoint Deployment Conundrum: On-premises, Cloud or Hybrid?

<--- Score

81. How much detail?

<--- Score

82. How do you know you are talking to the right device?

<--- Score

83. What type of support will be provided by each line of support?

<--- Score

84. How does microsoft handle your security and privacy?

<--- Score

85. Which users have access to what information?

<--- Score

86. What can you expect to happen?

<--- Score

87. How do you set a default view for all of your e-mail folders?

<--- Score

88. What services are offered for migrating from on-premises SharePoint to Office 365?

<--- Score

89. What functionality is your organization looking to obtain from an e-mail archiving capability?
<--- Score

90. What services are offered for migrating existing, on-premise Exchange mailboxes and email security settings to Office 365?
<--- Score

91. Which hybrid topology should you use?
<--- Score

92. What are the business pain points?
<--- Score

93. Does any application have any insider threat detection and response capability?
<--- Score

94. Modules are available that you may want?
<--- Score

95. Does your organization maintain a list of persons not eligible for service?
<--- Score

96. How do you deploy it?
<--- Score

97. Which of the above people would you expect to pay the highest insurance premiums?
<--- Score

98. Are room reservations/scheduling available in

Office 365?

<--- Score

99. Where can you get help and support?

<--- Score

100. Does the system model describe a large or a small enterprise, with a simple or a complex scheme of production?

<--- Score

101. How does office 365 support public folders?

<--- Score

102. Does the search experience differ in older versus newer logs?

<--- Score

103. How do you access the audit and security logs?

<--- Score

104. What is the file storage quota for SharePoint Online?

<--- Score

105. What are the limits of authorization?

<--- Score

106. Will vaulted items be migrated to the new mailbox in Office 365?

<--- Score

107. Does your organization comply with regulations related to federal funding sources?

<--- Score

108. How do you know what an incident is or when it is appropriate to perform a post-incident review?
<--- Score

109. What else is in office 365 for email users?
<--- Score

110. What are your top concerns when it comes to storage?
<--- Score

111. How does the system behave?
<--- Score

112. Do you have business operations that SharePoint could enhance?
<--- Score

113. Do you have an incident response workflow in place to remediate a situation?
<--- Score

114. Will all your current email be migrated to the new mailbox in Office 365?
<--- Score

115. How is the system structured?
<--- Score

116. Who provides primary support?
<--- Score

117. Who determines governance policies?
<--- Score

118. What are the rights and responsibilities of both the consumer and the insurance organization?

<--- Score

119. How do you set security policies?

<--- Score

120. What are the alternatives?

<--- Score

121. Who or what perceives/experiences the value of an attribute?

<--- Score

122. At what level of maturity would you classify your organizations technical capabilities?

<--- Score

123. What is application access and single sign-on with Azure Active Directory?

<--- Score

124. What portable media encryption product or pre-encrypted portable media products do you use?

<--- Score

125. Are you switching to cloud-based Microsoft Office 365 technology?

<--- Score

126. What should you actually do to help ensure that your environment is secure?

<--- Score

127. When a user gets stuck, who do they call?

<--- Score

128. Will the security of Dynamics 365 be synced with SharePoint?

<--- Score

129. Are public cloud apps/SaaS (such as Salesforce and Office 365) more or less secure than on-premises applications?

<--- Score

130. Accuracy: is the information accurate?

<--- Score

131. Have you made any errors in the Flow expressions that you have entered?

<--- Score

132. How much employee training have you been able to implement in order to increase product knowledge?

<--- Score

133. Generating and managing content in multiple SharePoint sites may lead one to question, How do you best find all relevant information?

<--- Score

134. How can you access a shared resource that is not migrated yet?

<--- Score

135. What is the sentiment on products compared to competitors in the web and on social media?

<--- Score

136. Do you have the resources?
<--- Score

137. What do you know about your end users (e.g., challenges, technical skills, etc.)?
<--- Score

138. How can it help?
<--- Score

139. How can or do licenses/subscriptions transfer?
<--- Score

140. Can field service be used for manufacturers who are doing own machine maintenance?
<--- Score

141. What are the biggest challenges your organization faces regarding ongoing support?
<--- Score

142. Who are your champions and why are they important?
<--- Score

143. How do you use powershell for performing operations in sharepoint?
<--- Score

144. How does the system operate?
<--- Score

145. Who else was brought in to help, and at what

time?
<--- Score

146. What happens if a structural link with dependency to a function is wrong?
<--- Score

147. What are your executive sponsors and why are they important?
<--- Score

148. What are the collaboration tools available in SharePoint?
<--- Score

149. Which are your main reasons for implementing SharePoint?
<--- Score

150. What licensing and consumption reporting will be available to Local Administrators?
<--- Score

151. Which patches, security policies, and firewall settings are continually updated?
<--- Score

152. How do you manage and respond to security alerts?
<--- Score

153. How will software licenses be systematically tracked and reported on while installed in various locations?
<--- Score

154. Will team members have the right to update inventory based on use rights granted through custom amendments?

<--- Score

155. How much backup storage and retention will you have?

<--- Score

156. What type of hardware firewalls will/do you employ?

<--- Score

157. Can you use an on-premises key management service to safeguard the encryption keys?

<--- Score

158. What is the general business purpose of this system?

<--- Score

159. What kinds of content can labels be applied to?

<--- Score

160. How secure and how reliable is office 365?

<--- Score

161. How do you secure this new world of IT?

<--- Score

162. If cutbacks in existing services are necessary, which services should be eliminated first?

<--- Score

163. Will flow be a separate license, and not

included in operations or other licenses?

<--- Score

164. Is the change management procedure being followed?

<--- Score

165. Can you use this with SharePoint?

<--- Score

166. How do you view the security state of your Azure resources?

<--- Score

167. What is the function/task/goal of the parts?

<--- Score

168. What information is in office 365, and how easily can it be shared?

<--- Score

169. Why did it make sense to take specific actions?

<--- Score

170. Where can you find details on Azure Security Center alerts?

<--- Score

171. What support services are available with the providers you are considering?

<--- Score

172. How do you use the Threat Intelligence Report?

<--- Score

173. The challenges of using an intrusion detection system: is it worth the effort?
<--- Score

174. Why is this important?
<--- Score

175. Will office be identical on a pc, a mac, and a mobile device?
<--- Score

176. Why are you using a tool more than an other?
<--- Score

177. What is the user experience if your organization does not have SharePoint in Office 365?
<--- Score

178. What is important for a conversation?
<--- Score

179. What type of applications must be integrated with SharePoint?
<--- Score

180. If you are migrating, what is the time frame?
<--- Score

181. What do you offer at this moment?
<--- Score

182. What do you want to communicate with the model?
<--- Score

183. How do you know sooner?
<--- Score

184. What existing SaaS platforms do you currently use?
<--- Score

185. Can an external user initiate an encrypted message to an internal user in Office 365?
<--- Score

186. Who is responsible for security?
<--- Score

187. Which authentication mechanism do you use?
<--- Score

188. Are user groups held to solicit software changes, and if so, how often?
<--- Score

189. What if the third-party shuts down its operations?
<--- Score

190. Is there a PIA for this system?
<--- Score

191. Model or not to model?
<--- Score

192. If you will be deploying hybrid search, in what time frame?
<--- Score

193. What do you want to achieve through your social media outreach and communication?

<--- Score

194. On which services or servers is e-mail?

<--- Score

195. Are the users satisfied with the performance and benefits of the IT Investment?

<--- Score

196. What does the public want to know?

<--- Score

197. Does that make sense for your enterprise and its use of Office 365?

<--- Score

198. How do you get started with external sharing for sharepoint online?

<--- Score

199. SharePoint user authentication and management: are all users employees found with the office 365 active directory environment?

<--- Score

200. What happens when an existing Microsoft NAV, Microsoft GP or Microsoft SL customer transitions from concurrent to named users?

<--- Score

201. Will room reservations/scheduling be available in Office 365?

<--- Score

202. Do you know how to fully leverage the rich set of APIs SharePoint provides for building new features or extending existing Enterprise Content Management (ECM) features?

<--- Score

203. How can you avoid manually provisioning servers that form part of a SharePoint Farm?

<--- Score

204. How do you structure permissions in a site?

<--- Score

205. Are new storage offerings, like object based storage or predictive storage, that your organization should include in storage or enhanced services?

<--- Score

206. What are you trying to accomplish?

<--- Score

207. What information in the system is PII?

<--- Score

208. Which are the system design alternatives?

<--- Score

209. How likely are you to have digital transformation conversations with customers that extend beyond Security & Compliance services?

<--- Score

210. How will cloud services change your business model?

<--- Score

211. What is the maximum acceptable delay before which temporary systems must be made available?

<--- Score

212. What happens when an employee leaves?

<--- Score

213. Does the GDPR apply to your organization?

<--- Score

214. Does this system/application interact with the public?

<--- Score

215. Do you have enough money to invest?

<--- Score

216. What are the key objectives for using Office 365?

<--- Score

217. What, if any, rules govern the physical location of the cloud service provision?

<--- Score

218. Should you enforce using a single tool?

<--- Score

219. How do you integrate with SharePoint applications that are not cloud ready?

<--- Score

220. What are your organizations challenges relating to communication and collaboration?

<--- Score

221. Is training available for Windows 10 and Office 365?
<--- Score

222. What flavor of SharePoint do you use?
<--- Score

223. What support do you have to create custom applications?
<--- Score

224. How do you want to categorize and manage your users by using SharePoint groups?
<--- Score

225. Do you have a comprehensive view of your licenses?
<--- Score

226. Will the sharepoint portal use an existing single sign-on system like ldap or active directory?
<--- Score

227. How do you figure out the right type, frequency, and mode of communication?
<--- Score

228. Does the project support your core businesses?
<--- Score

229. What is the physical interface between the parts?
<--- Score

230. What is the location of servers?
<--- Score

231. If a user becomes compromised, how can you configure security policies that automatically enforce additional layers of authentication to keep your organization safe?
<--- Score

232. What is important when maintaining the model?
<--- Score

233. How do you create rules?
<--- Score

234. What reason or reasons do you have for not having this item in the Replacement Value list?
<--- Score

235. How can you add greater value?
<--- Score

236. What browsers are supported?
<--- Score

237. If the schedule is less than 24 hours/day or 365 days/year, what limits the schedule to less than maximum?
<--- Score

238. Is there a preference to end user training or train the trainer?
<--- Score

239. Can sales professional and customer service enterprise be deployed on the same instance?
<--- Score

240. Which antivirus and malware protection software is implemented?
<--- Score

241. Is there a written change management procedure applicable?
<--- Score

242. Who has access to the information?
<--- Score

243. Which languages will be installed and supported?
<--- Score

244. How can you advise your customers if you only have pricing on the day of release?
<--- Score

245. How does your organization ensure that it is in compliance with federal and state employment laws?
<--- Score

246. What is the current number of deployed SharePoint users across the enterprise?
<--- Score

247. Why is your organization changing the way you work at this time?
<--- Score

248. Are archive folders backed up?
<--- Score

249. How do you know what is happening with the information?
<--- Score

250. What is the acceptable loss in functionality/ availability of your system?
<--- Score

251. What kind of content will you have on it?
<--- Score

252. What factors should you take into account in deciding on an investment strategy?
<--- Score

253. Can your application create specific accounts for people with no administrative rights (external auditors, non-IT executives, etc.), allowing them to perform audits securely and autonomously?
<--- Score

254. What reverse proxies are supported?
<--- Score

255. Are you using your current capacity efficiently?
<--- Score

256. Can you use External Sharing for SharePoint Online for your vendor/partner account?
<--- Score

257. How much time is lost from disjointed

security enforcement aimed at containing threats and protecting your organizations reputation?

<--- Score

258. Does upper management support the project effort?

<--- Score

259. Is there a written change management procedure?

<--- Score

260. Is it possible to create custom rules for generating alarms?

<--- Score

261. Block the infection vector - Which patches, security policies, and firewall settings should be continually updated?

<--- Score

262. What office productivity applications are installed with Office 365?

<--- Score

263. If you are considering automation tools, in what time frame?

<--- Score

264. What are the drawbacks of office 365?

<--- Score

265. Will there be test groups, and who will be in them?

<--- Score

266. Are you providing the highest level of service?

<--- Score

267. Why is the system built?

<--- Score

268. How will information be targeted at specific audiences?

<--- Score

269. Which service configuration do you use?

<--- Score

270. Are there any trade-offs?

<--- Score

271. Who is responsible for testing applications your organization uses with Windows 10 and Office 365?

<--- Score

272. Are you spending the right amount?

<--- Score

273. How do you want to use the model?

<--- Score

274. What is the time frame for migration?

<--- Score

275. What external and internal resources are assigned to enterprise architecture?

<--- Score

276. Does the application have Single Sign-On

(SSO)?

<--- Score

277. How do you balance security and productivity?

<--- Score

278. For finance and operations to automatically add the installation charge to sales orders. which three actions should you perform?

<--- Score

279. Will vendor/partner accounts be able to use the full functionality of Office 365 (Word Online / Excel online, etc.)?

<--- Score

280. What should the system affect?

<--- Score

281. What makes a system a system?

<--- Score

282. Why should this be accomplished?

<--- Score

283. Which applications are you currently hosting in the cloud?

<--- Score

284. On how many computers can you install Office 365?

<--- Score

285. What logs can you integrate?

<--- Score

286. Is there an option to participate only in the SharePoint contributor portion of Office 365?
<--- Score

287. What should be affected?
<--- Score

288. Which sharepoint users have access to what information in which sites?
<--- Score

289. How do you manage outages and downtime?
<--- Score

290. Are you using Microsoft SharePoint as an interface for Enterprise Applications?
<--- Score

291. What are the benefits of office 365?
<--- Score

292. How do you minimize your use of sensitive PII?
<--- Score

293. Which users have logged on to this endpoint?
<--- Score

294. What is a your secure environment?
<--- Score

295. How do you manage security incidents?
<--- Score

296. Is Augmented Reality code allowed in

sharepoint online?

<--- Score

297. How do you know what apps are used in your environment?

<--- Score

298. How do you want to share information within your organization?

<--- Score

299. Can you trust the operating system and the software that runs on it to be robust and secure?

<--- Score

300. Where are the encryption keys stored?

<--- Score

301. What is the desired effect?

<--- Score

302. How are your organizations of the attributes expressed?

<--- Score

303. Who are subject matter experts?

<--- Score

304. How can you access your SharePoint site off organization?

<--- Score

305. Expected # of units: how much of the service is purchased?

<--- Score

306. Is the users business environment stable?
<--- Score

307. Is your organization looking to archive information out of Microsoft SharePoint?
<--- Score

308. To achieve this goal, which component should you install on the computer connected to the cash drawer?
<--- Score

309. Is the synchronization in one direction or bi-directional (update anywhere)?
<--- Score

310. How can you serve your customers more effectively in the field?
<--- Score

311. When will your organization start paying for Windows 10 and Office 365?
<--- Score

312. Who is responsible for security in Office 365?
<--- Score

313. Do you have buy-in from all key stakeholders to make this transition successful?
<--- Score

314. What are the circumstances under which a client may be asked to no longer participate in services?
<--- Score

315. How will this service be managed and quality assured for your organization?
<--- Score

316. What are the rules for customer eligibility of the business edition?
<--- Score

317. Does this project have an incumbent?
<--- Score

318. What are the mandatory services related to SharePoint that have to be implemented in order to have a functioning system?
<--- Score

319. Which tool do you use?
<--- Score

320. What will be automatically calculated based on entering the dimensions of the packing box?
<--- Score

321. Which applications will remain on-premises?
<--- Score

322. What are the key attributes of a transition to cloud framework?
<--- Score

323. How, at the end of the day, do you really know that the content contains?
<--- Score

324. Are your records ok to stay where they are (In-Place) or should they reside within SharePoints

Records Center?
<--- Score

325. What is your incentive to move from on-premises to the cloud?
<--- Score

326. What is the target completion date for the entire project?
<--- Score

327. What are the mobile apps available for Operations?
<--- Score

328. At what minimally acceptable level of functionality can the enterprise operate?
<--- Score

329. Account for how could you protect yourself from something similar happening to you?
<--- Score

330. Are you be able to share/delegate calendar viewing in Office 365?
<--- Score

331. What does cloud app security provide?
<--- Score

332. Holistically what do you want SharePoint to achieve for your business?
<--- Score

333. How many client access licenses (CALs) does your organization own for MOSS Enterprise?

<--- Score

334. How do you obtain training for your sales and technical teams?
<--- Score

335. How far can you go with SharePoint for Enterprise Content Management?
<--- Score

336. Is custom code allowed in SharePoint online?
<--- Score

337. How do you address regulatory mandates?
<--- Score

338. Does the qa function have an appropriate level of independence from project management?
<--- Score

339. How is the product structure decomposed?
<--- Score

340. How do you manage your information?
<--- Score

341. Does your organization use an intranet such as SharePoint as your information hub?
<--- Score

342. Integrating the power of SharePoint - are you using SharePoint for storage only?
<--- Score

343. SharePoint: what version of office 365 licensing will be used?

<--- Score

344. Within the next twelve months, will you be migrating from your current SharePoint version?
<--- Score

345. What information (resources) is (should be) exchanged between stakeholders?
<--- Score

346. How can you make sure your business is providing the right message, to the right customer, at the right time, via the right channel?
<--- Score

347. Are any particular areas that you would like you to include in the training in particular?
<--- Score

348. What else can you do in sharepoint?
<--- Score

349. What level of availability does the service offer?
<--- Score

350. How do you go about completing an upgrade?
<--- Score

351. What procedures do you take when clients do not follow policy?
<--- Score

352. How will security be handled and who will be responsible for what?

<--- Score

353. What options are available if your organization prefers to migrate to Windows 10 and Office 365 later?
<--- Score

354. Do you want to allow requests to join/leave the group?
<--- Score

355. What one key skill do you possess that makes you an excellent marketer?
<--- Score

356. How will you be notified of security incidents?
<--- Score

357. Once a security incident is confirmed, what is the response?
<--- Score

358. Who manages the applications and infrastructure you have today?
<--- Score

359. Who has the power to kill the project?
<--- Score

360. How do you know if your users have been breached?
<--- Score

Add up total points for this section:
_ _ _ _ _ = Total points for this section

Divided by: _____ (number of
statements answered) = _____
Average score for this section

Transfer your score to the SharePoint
Online Office 365 Index at the
beginning of the Self-Assessment.

SharePoint Online Office 365 and Managing Projects, Criteria for Project Managers:

1.0 Initiating Process Group: SharePoint Online Office 365

1. When are the deliverables to be generated in each phase?

2. Mitigate. what will you do to minimize the impact should the risk event occur?

3. First of all, should any action be taken?

4. During which stage of Risk planning are modeling techniques used to determine overall effects of risks on SharePoint Online Office 365 project objectives for high probability, high impact risks?

5. How should needs be met?

6. Are you just doing busywork to pass the time?

7. Who supports, improves, and oversees standardized processes related to the SharePoint Online Office 365 projects program?

8. Were resources available as planned?

9. What will be the pressing issues of tomorrow?

10. Who does what?

11. What is the stake of others in your SharePoint Online Office 365 project?

12. The process to Manage Stakeholders is part of which process group?

13. Are there resources to maintain and support the outcome of the SharePoint Online Office 365 project?

14. Are stakeholders properly informed about the status of the SharePoint Online Office 365 project?

15. Are you properly tracking the progress of the SharePoint Online Office 365 project and communicating the status to stakeholders?

16. Does it make any difference if you am successful?

17. The SharePoint Online Office 365 project you are managing has nine stakeholders. How many channel of communications are there between corresponding stakeholders?

18. What are the short and long term implications?

19. In which SharePoint Online Office 365 project management process group is the detailed SharePoint Online Office 365 project budget created?

20. Just how important is your work to the overall success of the SharePoint Online Office 365 project?

1.1 Project Charter: SharePoint Online Office 365

21. Environmental stewardship and sustainability considerations: what is the process that will be used to ensure compliance with the environmental stewardship policy?

22. Will this replace an existing product?

23. For whom?

24. What is the business need?

25. What are the constraints?

26. What is the most common tool for helping define the detail?

27. Why executive support?

28. Is time of the essence?

29. Major high-level milestone targets: what events measure progress?

30. What barriers do you predict to your success?

31. When?

32. Name and describe the elements that deal with providing the detail?

33. How are SharePoint Online Office 365 projects different from operations?

34. Are you building in-house ?

35. What are the deliverables?

36. Run it as as a startup?

37. What material?

38. Market – identify products market, including whether it is outside of the objective: what is the purpose of the program or SharePoint Online Office 365 project?

39. Must Have?

40. Fit with other Products Compliments – Cannibalizes?

1.2 Stakeholder Register: SharePoint Online Office 365

41. What & Why?

42. How big is the gap?

43. Who is managing stakeholder engagement?

44. How should employers make voices heard?

45. Is your organization ready for change?

46. What opportunities exist to provide communications?

47. How much influence do they have on the SharePoint Online Office 365 project?

48. What is the power of the stakeholder?

49. Who are the stakeholders?

50. Who wants to talk about Security?

51. What are the major SharePoint Online Office 365 project milestones requiring communications or providing communications opportunities?

52. How will reports be created?

1.3 Stakeholder Analysis Matrix: SharePoint Online Office 365

53. Morale, commitment, leadership?

54. Who can contribute financial or technical resources towards the work?

55. Sustainable financial backing?

56. Insurmountable weaknesses?

57. Cashflow, start-up cash-drain?

58. If you can not fix it, how do you do it differently?

59. What is your Risk Management?

60. Who has not been involved up to now and should have been?

61. What do you Evaluate?

62. Has there been a similar initiative in the region?

63. What is the stakeholders name, what is function?

64. Are there different rules or organizational models for men and women?

65. What is in it for you?

66. Guiding question: who shall you involve in the

making of the stakeholder map?

67. If the baseline is now, and if its improved it will be better than now?

68. Disadvantages of proposition?

69. Why involve the stakeholder?

70. Who is most interested in information about the topic and/or has previously initiated interest?

71. How can you counter negative efforts?

72. Competitor intentions - various?

2.0 Planning Process Group: SharePoint Online Office 365

73. Will the products created live up to the necessary quality?

74. What is the critical path for this SharePoint Online Office 365 project, and what is the duration of the critical path?

75. Does it make any difference if you are successful?

76. If a risk event occurs, what will you do?

77. Is the schedule for the set products being met?

78. Have operating capacities been created and/or reinforced in partners?

79. How will users learn how to use the deliverables?

80. If a task is partitionable, is this a sufficient condition to reduce the SharePoint Online Office 365 project duration?

81. Why is it important to determine activity sequencing on SharePoint Online Office 365 projects?

82. What is the NEXT thing to do?

83. How well defined and documented are the SharePoint Online Office 365 project management processes you chose to use?

84. In which SharePoint Online Office 365 project management process group is the detailed SharePoint Online Office 365 project budget created?

85. Are the necessary foundations in place to ensure the sustainability of the results of the SharePoint Online Office 365 project?

86. How do you integrate SharePoint Online Office 365 project Planning with the Iterative/Evolutionary SDLC?

87. To what extent are the participating departments coordinating with each other?

88. How can you tell when you are done?

89. What will you do to minimize the impact should a risk event occur?

90. What are the different approaches to building the WBS?

91. To what extent has the intervention strategy been adapted to the areas of intervention in which it is being implemented?

92. What is the difference between the early schedule and late schedule?

2.1 Project Management Plan: SharePoint Online Office 365

93. What data/reports/tools/etc. do your PMs need?

94. Why do you manage integration?

95. If the SharePoint Online Office 365 project is complex or scope is specialized, do you have appropriate and/or qualified staff available to perform the tasks?

96. Why Change?

97. Are there any client staffing expectations?

98. Has the selected plan been formulated using cost effectiveness and incremental analysis techniques?

99. Are alternatives safe, functional, constructible, economical, reasonable and sustainable?

100. What data/reports/tools/etc. do program managers need?

101. How well are you able to manage your risk?

102. Was the peer (technical) review of the cost estimates duly coordinated with the cost estimate center of expertise and addressed in the review documentation and certification?

103. What went wrong?

104. Are comparable cost estimates used for comparing, screening and selecting alternative plans, and has a reasonable cost estimate been developed for the recommended plan?

105. Do the proposed changes from the SharePoint Online Office 365 project include any significant risks to safety?

106. What worked well?

107. What is risk management?

108. Is mitigation authorized or recommended?

109. What are the known stakeholder requirements?

2.2 Scope Management Plan: SharePoint Online Office 365

110. Have all team members been part of identifying risks?

111. Are the appropriate IT resources adequate to meet planned commitments?

112. Are corrective actions and variances reported?

113. Is each item clearly and completely defined?

114. Are risk triggers captured?

115. Organizational policies that might affect the availability of resources?

116. Is the steering committee active in SharePoint Online Office 365 project oversight?

117. What problem is being solved by delivering this SharePoint Online Office 365 project?

118. Alignment to strategic goals & objectives?

119. What are the risks that could significantly affect procuring consultant staff for the SharePoint Online Office 365 project?

120. Is there an onboarding process in place?

121. Has the schedule been baselined?

122. Has a structured approach been used to break work effort into manageable components (WBS)?

123. Are SharePoint Online Office 365 project leaders committed to this SharePoint Online Office 365 project full time?

124. Are multiple estimation methods being employed?

125. Do you keep stake holders informed?

126. Organizational unit (e.g., department, team, or person) who will accept responsibility for satisfactory completion of the item?

127. Does a documented SharePoint Online Office 365 project organizational policy & plan (i.e. governance model) exist?

128. Is the quality assurance team identified?

129. Does the SharePoint Online Office 365 project have a Statement of Work?

2.3 Requirements Management Plan: SharePoint Online Office 365

130. Do you have price sheets and a methodology for determining the total proposal cost?

131. How will unresolved questions be handled once approval has been obtained?

132. Who will do the reporting and to whom will reports be delivered?

133. Did you get proper approvals?

134. Who will initially review the SharePoint Online Office 365 project work or products to ensure it meets the applicable acceptance criteria?

135. How knowledgeable is the team in the proposed application area?

136. Do you have an agreed upon process for alerting the SharePoint Online Office 365 project Manager if a request for change in requirements leads to a product scope change?

137. Who has the authority to reject SharePoint Online Office 365 project requirements?

138. Will the product release be stable and mature enough to be deployed in the user community?

139. Should you include sub-activities?

140. Does the SharePoint Online Office 365 project have a Change Control process?

141. Is requirements work dependent on any other specific SharePoint Online Office 365 project or non-SharePoint Online Office 365 project activities (e.g. funding, approvals, procurement)?

142. Do you have an appropriate arrangement for meetings?

143. Who is responsible for quantifying the SharePoint Online Office 365 project requirements?

144. How detailed should the SharePoint Online Office 365 project get?

145. Is any organizational data being used or stored?

146. What performance metrics will be used?

147. Who is responsible for monitoring and tracking the SharePoint Online Office 365 project requirements?

148. The wbs is developed as part of a joint planning session. and how do you know that youhave done this right?

149. Is there formal agreement on who has authority to request a change in requirements?

2.4 Requirements Documentation: SharePoint Online Office 365

150. Is new technology needed?

151. How to document system requirements?

152. If applicable; are there issues linked with the fact that this is an offshore SharePoint Online Office 365 project?

153. Is your business case still valid?

154. Does the system provide the functions which best support the customers needs?

155. What is effective documentation?

156. Are all functions required by the customer included?

157. How will they be documented / shared?

158. Does your organization restrict technical alternatives?

159. How will the proposed SharePoint Online Office 365 project help?

160. Who is interacting with the system?

161. What are the potential disadvantages/ advantages?

162. Where do you define what is a customer, what are the attributes of customer?

163. How can you document system requirements?

164. Can you check system requirements?

165. What is the risk associated with the technology?

166. Do technical resources exist?

167. Who provides requirements?

168. How will requirements be documented and who signs off on them?

169. How does the proposed SharePoint Online Office 365 project contribute to the overall objectives of your organization?

2.5 Requirements Traceability Matrix: SharePoint Online Office 365

170. Will you use a Requirements Traceability Matrix?

171. Is there a requirements traceability process in place?

172. How do you manage scope?

173. Do you have a clear understanding of all subcontracts in place?

174. Why do you manage scope?

175. Describe the process for approving requirements so they can be added to the traceability matrix and SharePoint Online Office 365 project work can be performed. Will the SharePoint Online Office 365 project requirements become approved in writing?

176. What percentage of SharePoint Online Office 365 projects are producing traceability matrices between requirements and other work products?

177. How will it affect the stakeholders personally in career?

178. Why use a WBS?

179. What is the WBS?

180. How small is small enough?

181. What are the chronologies, contingencies, consequences, criteria?

2.6 Project Scope Statement: SharePoint Online Office 365

182. Is there a Quality Assurance Plan documented and filed?

183. Is the plan for SharePoint Online Office 365 project resources adequate?

184. If there is an independent oversight contractor, have they signed off on the SharePoint Online Office 365 project Plan?

185. What actions will be taken to mitigate the risk?

186. Once its defined, what is the stability of the SharePoint Online Office 365 project scope?

187. What went right?

188. If the scope changes, what will the impact be to your SharePoint Online Office 365 project in terms of duration, cost, quality, or any other important areas of the SharePoint Online Office 365 project?

189. Is there an information system for the SharePoint Online Office 365 project?

190. Will all tasks resulting from issues be entered into the SharePoint Online Office 365 project Plan and tracked through the plan?

191. Is an issue management process documented

and filed?

192. How will you verify the accuracy of the work of the SharePoint Online Office 365 project, and what constitutes acceptance of the deliverables?

193. Will tasks be marked complete only after QA has been successfully completed?

194. Have you been able to thoroughly document the SharePoint Online Office 365 projects assumptions and constraints?

195. Elements that deal with providing the detail?

196. Do you anticipate new stakeholders joining the SharePoint Online Office 365 project over time?

197. Will the risk plan be updated on a regular and frequent basis?

198. Is the change control process documented and on file?

199. Are the input requirements from the team members clearly documented and communicated?

200. SharePoint Online Office 365 project lead, team lead, solution architect?

201. Change management vs. change leadership - what is the difference?

2.7 Assumption and Constraint Log: SharePoint Online Office 365

202. Does the document/deliverable meet general requirements (for example, statement of work) for all deliverables?

203. Would known impacts serve as impediments?

204. Is the amount of effort justified by the anticipated value of forming a new process?

205. What is positive about the current process?

206. Were the system requirements formally reviewed prior to initiating the design phase?

207. Are there cosmetic errors that hinder readability and comprehension?

208. Is this process still needed?

209. Violation trace: why ?

210. What do you audit?

211. Does a specific action and/or state that is known to violate security policy occur?

212. Have all involved stakeholders and work groups committed to the SharePoint Online Office 365 project?

213. How many SharePoint Online Office 365 project staff does this specific process affect?

214. Is the current scope of the SharePoint Online Office 365 project substantially different than that originally defined in the approved SharePoint Online Office 365 project plan?

215. What to do at recovery?

216. What if failure during recovery?

217. Can you perform this task or activity in a more effective manner?

218. Contradictory information between document sections?

219. What would you gain if you spent time working to improve this process?

220. Has the approach and development strategy of the SharePoint Online Office 365 project been defined, documented and accepted by the appropriate stakeholders?

2.8 Work Breakdown Structure: SharePoint Online Office 365

221. Where does it take place?

222. Is it still viable?

223. When do you stop?

224. Who has to do it?

225. How far down?

226. Is it a change in scope?

227. What is the probability that the SharePoint Online Office 365 project duration will exceed xx weeks?

228. Can you make it?

229. How much detail?

230. Is the work breakdown structure (wbs) defined and is the scope of the SharePoint Online Office 365 project clear with assigned deliverable owners?

231. How big is a work-package?

232. When does it have to be done?

233. Do you need another level?

234. Why is it useful?

235. Why would you develop a Work Breakdown Structure?

236. What is the probability of completing the SharePoint Online Office 365 project in less that xx days?

237. How many levels?

2.9 WBS Dictionary: SharePoint Online Office 365

238. Are indirect costs accumulated for comparison with the corresponding budgets?

239. Is future work which cannot be planned in detail subdivided to the extent practicable for budgeting and scheduling purposes?

240. What should you drop in order to add something new?

241. Are estimates developed by SharePoint Online Office 365 project personnel coordinated with the already stated responsible for overall management to determine whether required resources will be available according to revised planning?

242. Does the contractors system include procedures for measuring performance of the lowest level organization responsible for the control account?

243. Are retroactive changes to BCWS and BCWP prohibited except for correction of errors or for normal accounting adjustments?

244. Does the scheduling system provide for the identification of work progress against technical and other milestones, and also provide for forecasts of completion dates of scheduled work?

245. Changes in the current direct and SharePoint

Online Office 365 projected base?

246. Are data elements summarized through the functional organizational structure for progressively higher levels of management?

247. Are control accounts opened and closed based on the start and completion of work contained therein?

248. Appropriate work authorization documents which subdivide the contractual effort and responsibilities, within functional organizations?

249. What is wrong with this SharePoint Online Office 365 project?

250. Budgets assigned to major functional organizations?

251. Are all authorized tasks assigned to identified organizational elements?

252. Are the bases and rates for allocating costs from each indirect pool to commercial work consistent with the already stated used to allocate corresponding costs to Government contracts?

253. Do the lines of authority for incurring indirect costs correspond to the lines of responsibility for management control of the same components of costs?

254. Are the rates for allocating costs from each indirect cost pool to contracts updated as necessary to ensure a realistic monthly allocation of indirect

costs without significant year-end adjustments?

255. Budgets assigned to control accounts?

256. Knowledgeable SharePoint Online Office 365 projections of future performance?

257. What size should a work package be?

2.10 Schedule Management Plan: SharePoint Online Office 365

258. Have activity relationships and interdependencies within tasks been adequately identified?

259. Are the primary and secondary schedule tools defined?

260. Are decisions captured in a decisions log?

261. Are all activities logically sequenced?

262. Is the critical path valid?

263. Why conduct schedule analysis?

264. Are action items captured and managed?

265. What weaknesses do you have?

266. Are tasks tracked by hours?

267. Is the plan consistent with industry best practices?

268. Were stakeholders aware and supportive of the principles and practices of modern software estimation?

269. Are software metrics formally captured, analyzed and used as a basis for other SharePoint Online Office

365 project estimates?

270. Was your organizations estimating methodology being used and followed?

271. Is there an approved case?

272. What date will the task finish?

273. Does the SharePoint Online Office 365 project have a Quality Culture?

274. Does the schedule have reasonable float?

275. Are the activity durations realistic and at an appropriate level of detail for effective management?

276. Are the predecessor and successor relationships accurate?

277. List all schedule constraints here. Must the SharePoint Online Office 365 project be complete by a specified date?

2.11 Activity List: SharePoint Online Office 365

278. What are the critical bottleneck activities?

279. What went well?

280. Who will perform the work?

281. How much slack is available in the SharePoint Online Office 365 project?

282. When do the individual activities need to start and finish?

283. What will be performed?

284. What is the LF and LS for each activity?

285. What did not go as well?

286. In what sequence?

287. How will it be performed?

288. How should ongoing costs be monitored to try to keep the SharePoint Online Office 365 project within budget?

289. Can you determine the activity that must finish, before this activity can start?

290. What is the probability the SharePoint Online

Office 365 project can be completed in xx weeks?

291. How do you determine the late start (LS) for each activity?

292. For other activities, how much delay can be tolerated?

293. Are the required resources available or need to be acquired?

294. Is there anything planned that does not need to be here?

2.12 Activity Attributes: SharePoint Online Office 365

295. How many days do you need to complete the work scope with a limit of X number of resources?

296. Are the required resources available?

297. Activity: what is Missing?

298. Can more resources be added?

299. How much activity detail is required?

300. What is the general pattern here?

301. What is missing?

302. Activity: fair or not fair?

303. What conclusions/generalizations can you draw from this?

304. Can you re-assign any activities to another resource to resolve an over-allocation?

305. What is your organizations history in doing similar activities?

306. How many resources do you need to complete the work scope within a limit of X number of days?

307. Do you feel very comfortable with your

prediction?

308. Where else does it apply?

309. Why?

310. How do you manage time?

311. Were there other ways you could have organized the data to achieve similar results?

312. Resources to accomplish the work?

2.13 Milestone List: SharePoint Online Office 365

313. What is the market for your technology, product or service?

314. Usps (unique selling points)?

315. Timescales, deadlines and pressures?

316. Loss of key staff?

317. Can you derive how soon can the whole SharePoint Online Office 365 project finish?

318. How will the milestone be verified?

319. How late can the activity finish?

320. Describe your organizations strengths and core competencies. What factors will make your organization succeed?

321. Vital contracts and partners?

322. Reliability of data, plan predictability?

323. How difficult will it be to do specific activities on this SharePoint Online Office 365 project?

324. Identify critical paths (one or more) and which activities are on the critical path?

325. It is to be a narrative text providing the crucial aspects of your SharePoint Online Office 365 project proposal answering what, who, how, when and where?

326. Information and research?

327. How will you get the word out to customers?

328. What has been done so far?

329. What specific improvements did you make to the SharePoint Online Office 365 project proposal since the previous time?

2.14 Network Diagram: SharePoint Online Office 365

330. What is the lowest cost to complete this SharePoint Online Office 365 project in xx weeks?

331. If a current contract exists, can you provide the vendor name, contract start, and contract expiration date?

332. What to do and When?

333. Why must you schedule milestones, such as reviews, throughout the SharePoint Online Office 365 project?

334. Can you calculate the confidence level?

335. Will crashing x weeks return more in benefits than it costs?

336. Review the logical flow of the network diagram. Take a look at which activities you have first and then sequence the activities. Do they make sense?

337. Planning: who, how long, what to do?

338. What job or jobs precede it?

339. Are you on time?

340. Are the gantt chart and/or network diagram updated periodically and used to assess the overall

SharePoint Online Office 365 project timetable?

341. What job or jobs follow it?

342. What job or jobs could run concurrently?

343. What is the probability of completing the SharePoint Online Office 365 project in less that xx days?

344. What are the Key Success Factors?

345. What controls the start and finish of a job?

346. What activities must occur simultaneously with this activity?

2.15 Activity Resource Requirements: SharePoint Online Office 365

347. Anything else?

348. Time for overtime?

349. What is the Work Plan Standard?

350. When does monitoring begin?

351. Organizational Applicability?

352. Why do you do that?

353. What are constraints that you might find during the Human Resource Planning process?

354. How many signatures do you require on a check and does this match what is in your policy and procedures?

355. Which logical relationship does the PDM use most often?

356. Other support in specific areas?

357. Do you use tools like decomposition and rolling-wave planning to produce the activity list and other outputs?

358. Are there unresolved issues that need to be addressed?

359. How do you handle petty cash?

2.16 Resource Breakdown Structure: SharePoint Online Office 365

360. What is each stakeholders desired outcome for the SharePoint Online Office 365 project?

361. Why time management?

362. Changes based on input from stakeholders?

363. Who needs what information?

364. What is the difference between % Complete and % work?

365. What can you do to improve productivity?

366. Who will use the system?

367. Any changes from stakeholders?

368. Who is allowed to see what data about which resources?

369. How should the information be delivered?

370. What is SharePoint Online Office 365 project communication management?

371. How can this help you with team building?

372. The list could probably go on, but, the thing that you would most like to know is, How long & How

much?

373. Goals for the SharePoint Online Office 365 project. What is each stakeholders desired outcome for the SharePoint Online Office 365 project?

374. Which resource planning tool provides information on resource responsibility and accountability?

2.17 Activity Duration Estimates: SharePoint Online Office 365

375. Which skills do you think are most important for an information technology SharePoint Online Office 365 project manager?

376. Is the SharePoint Online Office 365 project performing better or worse than planned?

377. What are the main parts of a scope statement?

378. How can software assist in SharePoint Online Office 365 project communications?

379. What are key inputs and outputs of the software?

380. What is the career outlook for SharePoint Online Office 365 project managers in information technology?

381. What is the difference between using brainstorming and the Delphi technique for risk identification?

382. How have experts such as Deming, Juran, Crosby, and Taguchi affected the quality movement and todays use of Six Sigma?

383. After changes are approved are SharePoint Online Office 365 project documents updated and distributed?

384. Does a process exist to identify SharePoint Online Office 365 project roles, responsibilities and reporting relationships?

385. Consider the examples of poor quality in information technology SharePoint Online Office 365 projects presented in the What Went Wrong?

386. Which is correct?

387. Are procurement documents used to solicit accurate and complete proposals from prospective sellers?

388. Consider the changes in the job market for information technology workers. How does the job market and current state of the economy affect human resource management?

389. How can others help SharePoint Online Office 365 project managers understand your organizational context for SharePoint Online Office 365 projects?

390. Why is it difficult to use SharePoint Online Office 365 project management software well?

391. What are the largest companies that provide information technology outsourcing services?

392. How many different communications channels does a SharePoint Online Office 365 project team with six people have?

393. Did anything besides luck make a difference between success and failure?

394. Briefly summarize the work done by Maslow, Herzberg, McClellan, McGregor, Ouchi, Thamhain and Wilemon, and Covey. How do theories relate to SharePoint Online Office 365 project management?

2.18 Duration Estimating Worksheet: SharePoint Online Office 365

395. How should ongoing costs be monitored to try to keep the SharePoint Online Office 365 project within budget?

396. What is next?

397. Will the SharePoint Online Office 365 project collaborate with the local community and leverage resources?

398. Why estimate time and cost?

399. What questions do you have?

400. Define the work as completely as possible. What work will be included in the SharePoint Online Office 365 project?

401. What is the total time required to complete the SharePoint Online Office 365 project if no delays occur?

402. What utility impacts are there?

403. Value pocket identification & quantification what are value pockets?

404. What is your role?

405. Why estimate costs?

406. What is an Average SharePoint Online Office 365 project?

407. What info is needed?

408. Is a construction detail attached (to aid in explanation)?

409. How can the SharePoint Online Office 365 project be displayed graphically to better visualize the activities?

410. Is this operation cost effective?

411. When does your organization expect to be able to complete it?

2.19 Project Schedule: SharePoint Online Office 365

412. Are procedures defined by which the SharePoint Online Office 365 project schedule may be changed?

413. What is the difference?

414. SharePoint Online Office 365 project work estimates Who is managing the work estimate quality of work tasks in the SharePoint Online Office 365 project schedule?

415. Are activities connected because logic dictates the order in which others occur?

416. Are all remaining durations correct?

417. To what degree is do you feel the entire team was committed to the SharePoint Online Office 365 project schedule?

418. What is the most mis-scheduled part of process?

419. Is the SharePoint Online Office 365 project schedule available for all SharePoint Online Office 365 project team members to review?

420. Why do you need to manage SharePoint Online Office 365 project Risk?

421. What is the purpose of a SharePoint Online Office 365 project schedule?

422. How can you shorten the schedule?

423. Did the SharePoint Online Office 365 project come in on schedule?

424. Is infrastructure setup part of your SharePoint Online Office 365 project?

425. Change management required?

426. How can you minimize or control changes to SharePoint Online Office 365 project schedules?

427. What does that mean?

428. How detailed should a SharePoint Online Office 365 project get?

429. Verify that the update is accurate. Are all remaining durations correct?

2.20 Cost Management Plan: SharePoint Online Office 365

430. Is the communication plan being followed?

431. Is pert / critical path or equivalent methodology being used?

432. Are vendor contract reports, reviews and visits conducted periodically?

433. Are quality inspections and review activities listed in the SharePoint Online Office 365 project schedule(s)?

434. Progress measurement and control – How will the SharePoint Online Office 365 project measure and control progress?

435. Is there any form of automated support for Issues Management?

436. Are updated SharePoint Online Office 365 project time & resource estimates reasonable based on the current SharePoint Online Office 365 project stage?

437. How do you manage cost?

438. Does the SharePoint Online Office 365 project have a Statement of Work?

439. Who will prepare the cost estimates?

440. Risk rating?

441. What would you do differently what did not work?

442. Contingency – how will cost contingency be administered?

443. Pareto diagrams, statistical sampling, flow charting or trend analysis used quality monitoring?

444. Sensitivity analysis?

445. Are all key components of a Quality Assurance Plan present?

446. Schedule preparation – how will the schedules be prepared during each phase of the SharePoint Online Office 365 project?

447. Environmental management – what changes in statutory environmental compliance requirements are anticipated during the SharePoint Online Office 365 project?

448. Is a payment system in place with proper reviews and approvals?

2.21 Activity Cost Estimates: SharePoint Online Office 365

449. Maintenance Reserve?

450. Will you need to provide essential services information about activities?

451. Scope statement only direct or indirect costs as well?

452. Can you delete activities or make them inactive?

453. How do you do activity recasts?

454. Are cost subtotals needed?

455. Will you use any tools, such as SharePoint Online Office 365 project management software, to assist in capturing Earned Value metrics?

456. What is procurement?

457. Were sponsors and decision makers available when needed outside regularly scheduled meetings?

458. What is the last item a SharePoint Online Office 365 project manager must do to finalize SharePoint Online Office 365 project close-out?

459. Who determines when the contractor is paid?

460. Did the SharePoint Online Office 365 project

team have the right skills?

461. Did the consultant work with local staff to develop local capacity?

462. What is SharePoint Online Office 365 project cost management?

463. What is the activity inventory?

464. Were the tasks or work products prepared by the consultant useful?

465. Estimated cost?

466. Based on your SharePoint Online Office 365 project communication management plan, what worked well?

467. How do you treat administrative costs in the activity inventory?

2.22 Cost Estimating Worksheet: SharePoint Online Office 365

468. What costs are to be estimated?

469. Who is best positioned to know and assist in identifying corresponding factors?

470. Is the SharePoint Online Office 365 project responsive to community need?

471. Ask: are others positioned to know, are others credible, and will others cooperate?

472. Identify the timeframe necessary to monitor progress and collect data to determine how the selected measure has changed?

473. Does the SharePoint Online Office 365 project provide innovative ways for stakeholders to overcome obstacles or deliver better outcomes?

474. Is it feasible to establish a control group arrangement?

475. What additional SharePoint Online Office 365 project(s) could be initiated as a result of this SharePoint Online Office 365 project?

476. What will others want?

477. Will the SharePoint Online Office 365 project collaborate with the local community and leverage

resources?

478. What is the estimated labor cost today based upon this information?

479. Can a trend be established from historical performance data on the selected measure and are the criteria for using trend analysis or forecasting methods met?

480. How will the results be shared and to whom?

481. What is the purpose of estimating?

482. What can be included?

483. What happens to any remaining funds not used?

2.23 Cost Baseline: SharePoint Online Office 365

484. Has the SharePoint Online Office 365 projected annual cost to operate and maintain the product(s) or service(s) been approved and funded?

485. What does a good WBS NOT look like?

486. SharePoint Online Office 365 project goals -should others be reconsidered?

487. Has the SharePoint Online Office 365 project (or SharePoint Online Office 365 project phase) been evaluated against each objective established in the product description and Integrated SharePoint Online Office 365 project Plan?

488. How long are you willing to wait before you find out were late?

489. Is the requested change request a result of changes in other SharePoint Online Office 365 project(s)?

490. Is the cr within SharePoint Online Office 365 project scope?

491. Eac -estimate at completion, what is the total job expected to cost?

492. Are you meeting with your team regularly?

493. Have you identified skills that are missing from your team?

494. How concrete were original objectives?

495. Are there contingencies or conditions related to the acceptance?

496. Have the resources used by the SharePoint Online Office 365 project been reassigned to other units or SharePoint Online Office 365 projects?

497. Review your risk triggers -have your risks changed?

498. What would the life cycle costs be?

499. What can go wrong?

500. Is there anything you need from upper management in order to be successful?

501. Does it impact schedule, cost, quality?

502. How will cost estimates be used?

503. Has the appropriate access to relevant data and analysis capability been granted?

2.24 Quality Management Plan: SharePoint Online Office 365

504. How relevant is this attribute to this SharePoint Online Office 365 project or audit?

505. Meet how often?

506. What are your organizations current levels and trends for the already stated measures related to financial and marketplace performance?

507. Are requirements management tracking tools and procedures in place?

508. Who needs a qmp?

509. Methodology followed?

510. Written by multiple authors and in multiple writing styles?

511. What are your organizations key processes (product, service, business, and support)?

512. Do the data quality objectives communicate the intended program need?

513. What are the appropriate test methods to be used?

514. What process do you use to minimize errors, defects, and rework?

515. How are your organizations compensation and recognition approaches and the performance management system used to reinforce high performance?

516. What are your organizations current levels and trends for the already stated measures related to customer satisfaction/ dissatisfaction and product/ service performance?

517. How is equipment calibrated?

518. Are there processes in place to ensure internal consistency between the source code components?

519. What changes can you make that will result in improvement?

520. What is the Difference Between a QMP and QAPP?

521. Results Available?

522. How is staff trained?

523. What is the return on investment?

2.25 Quality Metrics: SharePoint Online Office 365

524. Can visual measures help you to filter visualizations of interest?

525. What do you measure?

526. Which report did you use to create the data you are submitting?

527. What percentage are outcome-based?

528. There are many reasons to shore up quality-related metrics, and what metrics are important?

529. What metrics do you measure?

530. What are your organizations next steps?

531. What is the benchmark?

532. Did evaluation start on time?

533. Can you correlate your quality metrics to profitability?

534. Do you know how much profit a 10% decrease in waste would generate?

535. What makes a visualization memorable?

536. Are applicable standards referenced and

available?

537. How do you communicate results and findings to upper management?

538. Have risk areas been identified?

539. What documentation is required?

540. How do you calculate such metrics?

541. What method of measurement do you use?

542. Where did complaints, returns and warranty claims come from?

543. The metrics–what is being considered?

2.26 Process Improvement Plan: SharePoint Online Office 365

544. What personnel are the coaches for your initiative?

545. Has a process guide to collect the data been developed?

546. What lessons have you learned so far?

547. Are you making progress on the improvement framework?

548. What personnel are the sponsors for that initiative?

549. What personnel are the change agents for your initiative?

550. How do you measure?

551. Where are you now?

552. If a process improvement framework is being used, which elements will help the problems and goals listed?

553. Where do you want to be?

554. Modeling current processes is great, and will you ever see a return on that investment?

555. What is quality and how will you ensure it?

556. Where do you focus?

557. Are you making progress on your improvement plan?

558. Are you following the quality standards?

559. Does explicit definition of the measures exist?

560. What actions are needed to address the problems and achieve the goals?

561. Who should prepare the process improvement action plan?

562. Are you meeting the quality standards?

2.27 Responsibility Assignment Matrix: SharePoint Online Office 365

563. With too many people labeled as doing the work, are there too many hands involved?

564. Is the anticipated (firm and potential) business base SharePoint Online Office 365 projected in a rational, consistent manner?

565. Identify and isolate causes of favorable and unfavorable cost and schedule variances?

566. Are estimates of costs at completion generated in a rational, consistent manner?

567. Too many rs: with too many people labeled as doing the work, are there too many hands involved?

568. Too many is: do all the identified roles need to be routinely informed or only in exceptional circumstances?

569. No rs: if a task has no one listed as responsible, who is getting the job done?

570. Is the entire contract planned in time-phased control accounts to the extent practicable?

571. Does the contractor use objective results, design reviews, and tests to trace schedule?

572. Changes in the current direct and SharePoint

Online Office 365 projected base?

573. Contract line items and end items?

574. Is every signing-off responsibility and every communicating responsibility critically necessary?

575. Most people let you know when others re too busy, and are others really too busy?

576. What travel needed?

577. What do you need to implement earned value management?

578. Is accountability placed at the lowest-possible level within the SharePoint Online Office 365 project so that decisions can be made at that level?

579. What expertise is not available in your department?

580. Past experience – the person or the group worked at something similar in the past?

2.28 Roles and Responsibilities: SharePoint Online Office 365

581. What specific behaviors did you observe?

582. Are your budgets supportive of a culture of quality data?

583. Be specific; avoid generalities. Thank you and great work alone are insufficient. What exactly do you appreciate and why?

584. Are governance roles and responsibilities documented?

585. What is working well within your organizations performance management system?

586. Where are you most strong as a supervisor?

587. What expectations were met?

588. Concern: where are you limited or have no authority, where you can not influence?

589. How is your work-life balance?

590. What are your major roles and responsibilities in the area of performance measurement and assessment?

591. What should you do now to ensure that you are meeting all expectations of your current position?

592. Are your policies supportive of a culture of quality data?

593. Who is involved?

594. What should you highlight for improvement?

595. How well did the SharePoint Online Office 365 project Team understand the expectations of specific roles and responsibilities?

596. Who is responsible for each task?

597. Accountabilities: what are the roles and responsibilities of individual team members?

2.29 Human Resource Management Plan: SharePoint Online Office 365

598. Is your organization certified as a supplier, wholesaler, regular dealer, or manufacturer of corresponding products/supplies?

599. Are trade-offs between accepting the risk and mitigating the risk identified?

600. Is the SharePoint Online Office 365 project sponsor clearly communicating the business case or rationale for why this SharePoint Online Office 365 project is needed?

601. Is it possible to track all classes of SharePoint Online Office 365 project work (e.g. scheduled, unscheduled, defect repair, etc.)?

602. List the assumptions made to date. What did you have to assume to be true to complete the charter?

603. Responsiveness to change and the resulting demands for different skills and abilities?

604. Does the resource management plan include a personnel development plan?

605. How well does your organization communicate?

606. Did the SharePoint Online Office 365 project team have the right skills?

607. Is there a Steering Committee in place?

608. Is stakeholder involvement adequate?

609. Is the current culture aligned with the vision, mission, and values of the department?

610. What were things that you need to improve?

611. Are quality metrics defined?

612. Were SharePoint Online Office 365 project team members involved in the development of activity & task decomposition?

613. How complete is the human resource management plan?

614. Are changes in deliverable commitments agreed to by all affected groups & individuals?

2.30 Communications Management Plan: SharePoint Online Office 365

615. Do you feel a register helps?

616. What approaches to you feel are the best ones to use?

617. Who are the members of the governing body?

618. How is this initiative related to other portfolios, programs, or SharePoint Online Office 365 projects?

619. Who needs to know and how much?

620. What approaches do you use?

621. Is there an important stakeholder who is actively opposed and will not receive messages?

622. Are there common objectives between the team and the stakeholder?

623. How were corresponding initiatives successful?

624. Who is responsible?

625. Do you then often overlook a key stakeholder or stakeholder group?

626. Why manage stakeholders?

627. What is the political influence?

628. Do you prepare stakeholder engagement plans?

629. Which team member will work with each stakeholder?

630. How do you manage communications?

631. Why is stakeholder engagement important?

632. Are there potential barriers between the team and the stakeholder?

633. Are others needed?

2.31 Risk Management Plan: SharePoint Online Office 365

634. Are the reports useful and easy to read?

635. Are requirements fully understood by the software engineering team and customers?

636. How much risk protection can you afford?

637. What would you do?

638. Are you on schedule?

639. Number of users of the product?

640. Havent software SharePoint Online Office 365 projects been late before?

641. Was an original risk assessment/risk management plan completed?

642. Why might it be late?

643. Is the necessary data being captured and is it complete and accurate?

644. Can it be changed quickly?

645. Who should be notified of the occurrence of each of the indicators?

646. What will drive change?

647. Degree of confidence in estimated size estimate?

648. Do the people have the right combinations of skills?

649. Can the SharePoint Online Office 365 project proceed without assuming the risk?

650. Do you have a mechanism for managing change?

651. People risk -are people with appropriate skills available to help complete the SharePoint Online Office 365 project?

2.32 Risk Register: SharePoint Online Office 365

652. What is a Risk?

653. Are your objectives at risk?

654. What can be done about it?

655. What evidence do you have to justify the likelihood score of the risk (audit, incident report, claim, complaints, inspection, internal review)?

656. What should you do when?

657. Recovery actions - planned actions taken once a risk has occurred to allow you to move on. What should you do after?

658. Financial risk -can your organization afford to undertake the SharePoint Online Office 365 project?

659. Do you require further engagement?

660. Technology risk -is the SharePoint Online Office 365 project technically feasible?

661. Assume the risk event or situation happens, what would the impact be?

662. Are there any knock-on effects/impact on any of the other areas?

663. What is the reason for current performance gaps and do the risks and opportunities identified previously account for this?

664. User involvement: do you have the right users?

665. People risk -are people with appropriate skills available to help complete the SharePoint Online Office 365 project?

666. Are there other alternative controls that could be implemented?

667. Are corrective measures implemented as planned?

668. Severity Prediction?

669. What should the audit role be in establishing a risk management process?

670. How could corresponding Risk affect the SharePoint Online Office 365 project in terms of cost and schedule?

2.33 Probability and Impact Assessment: SharePoint Online Office 365

671. What are the channels available for distribution to the customer?

672. What action do you usually take against risks?

673. Have you ascribed a level of confidence to every critical technical objective?

674. What are the uncertainties associated with the technology selected for the SharePoint Online Office 365 project?

675. Are tools for analysis and design available?

676. How do risks change during the SharePoint Online Office 365 projects life cycle?

677. How would you assess the risk management process in the SharePoint Online Office 365 project?

678. Do you manage the process through use of metrics?

679. What will be the likely political situation during the life of the SharePoint Online Office 365 project?

680. Assumptions analysis -what assumptions have you made or been given about your SharePoint Online Office 365 project?

681. Should the risk be taken at all?

682. What risks does the employee encounter?

683. Are some people working on multiple SharePoint Online Office 365 projects?

684. Are the risk data complete?

685. Are flexibility and reuse paramount?

686. Are end-users enthusiastically committed to the SharePoint Online Office 365 project and the system/product to be built?

687. Do benefits and chances of success outweigh potential damage if success is not attained?

688. What are the likely future requirements?

689. How do you maximize short-term return on investment?

2.34 Probability and Impact Matrix: SharePoint Online Office 365

690. What kind of preparation would be required to do this?

691. What lifestyle shifts might occur in society?

692. How completely has the customer been identified?

693. What are the chances the event will occur?

694. How is the risk management process used in practice?

695. Is the customer willing to participate in reviews?

696. My SharePoint Online Office 365 project leader has suddenly left your organization, what do you do?

697. What will be the likely incidence of conflict with neighboring SharePoint Online Office 365 projects?

698. What is the risk appetite?

699. What risks are necessary to achieve success?

700. Is the process supported by tools?

701. Does the SharePoint Online Office 365 project team have experience with the technology to be implemented?

702. Which risks need to move on to Perform Quantitative Risk Analysis?

703. Have customers been involved fully in the definition of requirements?

704. During SharePoint Online Office 365 project executing, a team member identifies a risk that is not in the risk register. What should you do?

705. What is the level of experience available with your organization?

706. What are the uncertainties associated with the technology selected for the SharePoint Online Office 365 project?

707. Prioritized components/features?

708. How risk averse are you?

2.35 Risk Data Sheet: SharePoint Online Office 365

709. What are your core values?

710. What is the likelihood of it happening?

711. What is the chance that it will happen?

712. What will be the consequences if it happens?

713. What are you weak at and therefore need to do better?

714. How do you handle product safely?

715. Risk of what?

716. How can hazards be reduced?

717. What can you do?

718. During work activities could hazards exist?

719. How reliable is the data source?

720. Will revised controls lead to tolerable risk levels?

721. What is the environment within which you operate (social trends, economic, community values, broad based participation, national directions etc.)?

722. What was measured?

723. If it happens, what are the consequences?

724. What were the Causes that contributed?

725. What are you trying to achieve (Objectives)?

726. What actions can be taken to eliminate or remove risk?

727. What will be the consequences if the risk happens?

728. What are the main opportunities available to you that you should grab while you can?

2.36 Procurement Management Plan: SharePoint Online Office 365

729. Are the quality tools and methods identified in the Quality Plan appropriate to the SharePoint Online Office 365 project?

730. Are the people assigned to the SharePoint Online Office 365 project sufficiently qualified?

731. Is there a formal process for updating the SharePoint Online Office 365 project baseline?

732. Have the procedures for identifying budget variances been followed?

733. Are SharePoint Online Office 365 project team members committed fulltime?

734. Was the scope definition used in task sequencing?

735. Similar SharePoint Online Office 365 projects?

736. Are key risk mitigation strategies added to the SharePoint Online Office 365 project schedule?

737. If independent estimates will be needed as evaluation criteria, who will prepare them and when?

738. Have SharePoint Online Office 365 project team accountabilities & responsibilities been clearly defined?

739. Are any non-compliance issues that exist communicated to your organization?

740. Do you have the reasons why the changes to your organizational systems and capabilities are required?

741. Are all resource assumptions documented?

742. Is an industry recognized mechanized support tool(s) being used for SharePoint Online Office 365 project scheduling & tracking?

743. Are post milestone SharePoint Online Office 365 project reviews (PMPR) conducted with your organization at least once a year?

2.37 Source Selection Criteria: SharePoint Online Office 365

744. Does your documentation identify why the team concurs or differs with reported performance from past performance report (CPARs, questionnaire responses, etc.)?

745. What are the limitations on pre-competitive range communications?

746. If the costs are normalized, please account for how the normalization is conducted. Is a cost realism analysis used?

747. Can you identify proposed teaming partners and/or subcontractors and consider the nature and extent of proposed involvement in satisfying the SharePoint Online Office 365 project requirements?

748. Are there any specific considerations that precludes offers from being selected as the awardee?

749. How should the preproposal conference be conducted?

750. Are evaluators ready to begin this task?

751. What should preproposal conferences accomplish?

752. Are they compliant with all technical requirements?

753. When is it appropriate to issue a Draft Request for Proposal (DRFP)?

754. How should the solicitation aspects regarding past performance be structured?

755. How much weight should be placed on past performance information?

756. Have all evaluators been trained?

757. What should a Draft Request for Proposal (DRFP) include?

758. How are clarifications and communications appropriately used?

759. Team leads: what is your process for assigning ratings?

760. Why promote competition?

761. How and when do you enter into SharePoint Online Office 365 project Procurement Management?

762. What can not be disclosed?

763. What information may not be provided?

2.38 Stakeholder Management Plan: SharePoint Online Office 365

764. Has a sponsor been identified?

765. Are adequate resources provided for the quality assurance function?

766. Who is responsible for arranging and managing the review(s)?

767. Which impacts could serve as impediments?

768. Are schedule deliverables actually delivered?

769. Are the payment terms being followed?

770. What are the criteria for selecting suppliers of off the shelf products?

771. How many SharePoint Online Office 365 project staff does this specific process affect?

772. Does the detailed work plan match the complexity of tasks with the capabilities of personnel?

773. Who is responsible for the post implementation review process?

774. Are written status reports provided on a designated frequent basis?

775. Are procurement deliverables arriving on time

and to specification?

776. Has a capability assessment been conducted?

777. Are there nonconformance issues?

778. Was trending evident between reviews?

779. Does the SharePoint Online Office 365 project have a formal SharePoint Online Office 365 project Charter?

2.39 Change Management Plan: SharePoint Online Office 365

780. When does it make sense to customize?

781. When to start change management?

782. Identify the risk and assess the significance and likelihood of it occurring and plan the contingency What risks may occur upfront?

783. How will you deal with anger about the restricting of communications due to confidentiality considerations?

784. What prerequisite knowledge or training is required?

785. What did the people around you say about it?

786. How many people are required in each of the roles?

787. Who might present the most resistance?

788. Who is the target audience of the piece of information?

789. Has the target training audience been identified and nominated?

790. Have the business unit contacts been briefed by the SharePoint Online Office 365 project team?

791. What new competencies will be required for the roles?

792. What does a resilient organization look like?

793. What prerequisite knowledge do corresponding groups need?

794. Is a training information sheet available?

795. Is there support for this application(s) and are the details available for distribution?

796. Has a training need analysis been carried out?

797. Clearly articulate the overall business benefits of the SharePoint Online Office 365 project -why are you doing this now?

798. How much SharePoint Online Office 365 project management is needed?

799. Are there any restrictions on who can receive the communications?

3.0 Executing Process Group: SharePoint Online Office 365

800. Why do you need a good WBS to use SharePoint Online Office 365 project management software?

801. Could a new application negatively affect the current IT infrastructure?

802. What are the main parts of the scope statement?

803. Who are the SharePoint Online Office 365 project stakeholders?

804. What is the critical path for this SharePoint Online Office 365 project and how long is it?

805. What are deliverables of your SharePoint Online Office 365 project?

806. Would you rate yourself as being risk-averse, risk-neutral, or risk-seeking?

807. When will the SharePoint Online Office 365 project be done?

808. What are the main types of contracts if you do decide to outsource?

809. How can your organization use a weighted decision matrix to evaluate proposals as part of source selection?

810. What are the typical SharePoint Online Office 365 project management skills?

811. What factors are contributing to progress or delay in the achievement of products and results?

812. What type of people would you want on your team?

813. Do the products created live up to the necessary quality?

814. Why is it important to determine activity sequencing on SharePoint Online Office 365 projects?

815. What are the main processes included in SharePoint Online Office 365 project quality management?

816. How well did the team follow the chosen processes?

817. How is SharePoint Online Office 365 project performance information created and distributed?

3.1 Team Member Status Report: SharePoint Online Office 365

818. Is there evidence that staff is taking a more professional approach toward management of your organizations SharePoint Online Office 365 projects?

819. What is to be done?

820. How does this product, good, or service meet the needs of the SharePoint Online Office 365 project and your organization as a whole?

821. Will the staff do training or is that done by a third party?

822. The problem with Reward & Recognition Programs is that the truly deserving people all too often get left out. How can you make it practical?

823. Do you have an Enterprise SharePoint Online Office 365 project Management Office (EPMO)?

824. Are the attitudes of staff regarding SharePoint Online Office 365 project work improving?

825. Are the products of your organizations SharePoint Online Office 365 projects meeting customers objectives?

826. When a teams productivity and success depend on collaboration and the efficient flow of information, what generally fails them?

827. Does every department have to have a SharePoint Online Office 365 project Manager on staff?

828. How can you make it practical?

829. Are your organizations SharePoint Online Office 365 projects more successful over time?

830. Why is it to be done?

831. Does your organization have the means (staff, money, contract, etc.) to produce or to acquire the product, good, or service?

832. What specific interest groups do you have in place?

833. How will resource planning be done?

834. How much risk is involved?

835. How it is to be done?

836. Does the product, good, or service already exist within your organization?

3.2 Change Request: SharePoint Online Office 365

837. What needs to be communicated?

838. How are the measures for carrying out the change established?

839. Should staff call into the helpdesk or go to the website?

840. What are the Impacts to your organization?

841. Are there requirements attributes that can discriminate between high and low reliability?

842. Who needs to approve change requests?

843. How fast will change requests be approved?

844. What kind of information about the change request needs to be captured?

845. Who will perform the change?

846. Can you answer what happened, who did it, when did it happen, and what else will be affected?

847. Who is responsible to authorize changes?

848. What mechanism is used to appraise others of changes that are made?

849. Why do you want to have a change control system?

850. How do team members communicate with each other?

851. When to submit a change request?

852. Are there requirements attributes that are strongly related to the occurrence of defects and failures?

853. How many lines of code must be changed to implement the change?

854. Why control change across the life cycle?

855. Has the change been highlighted and documented in the CSCI?

856. How does your organization control changes before and after software is released to a customer?

3.3 Change Log: SharePoint Online Office 365

857. Who initiated the change request?

858. Is this a mandatory replacement?

859. How does this change affect the timeline of the schedule?

860. Is the change request within SharePoint Online Office 365 project scope?

861. Where do changes come from?

862. How does this relate to the standards developed for specific business processes?

863. Is the requested change request a result of changes in other SharePoint Online Office 365 project(s)?

864. Is the submitted change a new change or a modification of a previously approved change?

865. When was the request submitted?

866. Should a more thorough impact analysis be conducted?

867. Will the SharePoint Online Office 365 project fail if the change request is not executed?

868. When was the request approved?

869. Is the change request open, closed or pending?

870. Does the suggested change request seem to represent a necessary enhancement to the product?

871. Do the described changes impact on the integrity or security of the system?

872. How does this change affect scope?

873. Does the suggested change request represent a desired enhancement to the products functionality?

874. Is the change backward compatible without limitations?

3.4 Decision Log: SharePoint Online Office 365

875. Behaviors; what are guidelines that the team has identified that will assist them with getting the most out of team meetings?

876. It becomes critical to track and periodically revisit both operational effectiveness; Are you noticing all that you need to, and are you interpreting what you see effectively?

877. Meeting purpose; why does this team meet?

878. How does provision of information, both in terms of content and presentation, influence acceptance of alternative strategies?

879. Is your opponent open to a non-traditional workflow, or will it likely challenge anything you do?

880. How does an increasing emphasis on cost containment influence the strategies and tactics used?

881. Who will be given a copy of this document and where will it be kept?

882. What is your overall strategy for quality control / quality assurance procedures?

883. Is everything working as expected?

884. How effective is maintaining the log at facilitating organizational learning?

885. With whom was the decision shared or considered?

886. What alternatives/risks were considered?

887. Decision-making process; how will the team make decisions?

888. How do you define success?

889. What are the cost implications?

890. What eDiscovery problem or issue did your organization set out to fix or make better?

891. How does the use a Decision Support System influence the strategies/tactics or costs?

892. What was the rationale for the decision?

893. What is the line where eDiscovery ends and document review begins?

894. Which variables make a critical difference?

3.5 Quality Audit: SharePoint Online Office 365

895. Does your organization have set of goals, objectives, strategies and targets that are clearly understood by the Board and staff?

896. Do all staff have the necessary authority and resources to deliver what is expected of them?

897. How does your organization know that its financial management system is appropriately effective and constructive?

898. Does everyone know what they are supposed to be doing, how and why?

899. How does your organization know that it provides a safe and healthy environment?

900. Is there any content that may be legally actionable?

901. What is your organizations greatest strength?

902. How does your organization know that its system for recruiting the best staff possible are appropriately effective and constructive?

903. What is the collective experience of the team to be assigned to an audit?

904. How do staff know if they are doing a good job?

905. How does your organization know that its system for commercializing research outputs is appropriately effective and constructive?

906. How does your organization know that it is maintaining a conducive staff climate?

907. Do prior clients have a positive opinion of your organization?

908. How does your organization know that its management system is appropriately effective and constructive?

909. Are adequate and conveniently located toilet facilities available for use by the employees?

910. Are all complaints involving the possible failure of a device, labeling, or packaging to meet any of its specifications reviewed, evaluated, and investigated?

911. Does the audit organization have experience in performing the required work for entities of your type and size?

912. What mechanisms exist for identification of staff development needs?

913. Does the supplier use a formal quality system?

914. Are all records associated with the reconditioning of a device maintained for a minimum of two years after the sale or disposal of the last device within a lot of merchandise?

3.6 Team Directory: SharePoint Online Office 365

915. Days from the time the issue is identified?

916. What are you going to deliver or accomplish?

917. Contract requirements complied with?

918. Who will be the stakeholders on your next SharePoint Online Office 365 project?

919. Where should the information be distributed?

920. Who will write the meeting minutes and distribute?

921. Process decisions: are all start-up, turn over and close out requirements of the contract satisfied?

922. Who are your stakeholders (customers, sponsors, end users, team members)?

923. Process decisions: is work progressing on schedule and per contract requirements?

924. How and in what format should information be presented?

925. Who will talk to the customer?

926. Timing: when do the effects of communication take place?

927. How will you accomplish and manage the objectives?

928. When does information need to be distributed?

929. Who are the Team Members?

930. Does a SharePoint Online Office 365 project team directory list all resources assigned to the SharePoint Online Office 365 project?

931. Where will the product be used and/or delivered or built when appropriate?

932. Process decisions: are there any statutory or regulatory issues relevant to the timely execution of work?

3.7 Team Operating Agreement: SharePoint Online Office 365

933. Communication protocols: how will the team communicate?

934. Do you prevent individuals from dominating the meeting?

935. The method to be used in the decision making process; Will it be consensus, majority rule, or the supervisor having the final say?

936. What are the boundaries (organizational or geographic) within which you operate?

937. Do you call or email participants to ensure understanding, follow-through and commitment to the meeting outcomes?

938. Did you determine the technology methods that best match the messages to be communicated?

939. Did you prepare participants for the next meeting?

940. How will group handle unplanned absences?

941. Do you listen for voice tone and word choice to understand the meaning behind words?

942. Are there differences in access to communication and collaboration technology based on team member

location?

943. What is the anticipated procedure (recruitment, solicitation of volunteers, or assignment) for selecting team members?

944. Do you record meetings for the already stated unable to attend?

945. Do team members reside in more than two countries?

946. To whom do you deliver your services?

947. What are the current caseload numbers in the unit?

948. Do you leverage technology engagement tools group chat, polls, screen sharing, etc.?

949. Do you vary your voice pace, tone and pitch to engage participants and gain involvement?

950. Are team roles clearly defined and accepted?

951. Methodologies: how will key team processes be implemented, such as training, research, work deliverable production, review and approval processes, knowledge management, and meeting procedures?

3.8 Team Performance Assessment: SharePoint Online Office 365

952. Delaying market entry: how long is too long?

953. To what degree does the teams purpose contain themes that are particularly meaningful and memorable?

954. To what degree does the teams work approach provide opportunity for members to engage in fact-based problem solving?

955. How much interpersonal friction is there in your team?

956. To what degree are corresponding categories of skills either actually or potentially represented across the membership?

957. To what degree will new and supplemental skills be introduced as the need is recognized?

958. Does more radicalness mean more perceived benefits?

959. Do friends perform better than acquaintances?

960. To what degree can the team ensure that all members are individually and jointly accountable for the teams purpose, goals, approach, and work-products?

961. To what degree do all members feel responsible for all agreed-upon measures?

962. To what degree are fresh input and perspectives systematically caught and added (for example, through information and analysis, new members, and senior sponsors)?

963. To what degree are the goals realistic?

964. How do you manage human resources?

965. Can team performance be reliably measured in simulator and live exercises using the same assessment tool?

966. To what degree does the teams approach to its work allow for modification and improvement over time?

967. How do you keep key people outside the group informed about its accomplishments?

968. To what degree are staff involved as partners in the improvement process?

969. To what degree does the teams work approach provide opportunity for members to engage in results-based evaluation?

970. How hard did you try to make a good selection?

971. To what degree do the goals specify concrete team work products?

3.9 Team Member Performance Assessment: SharePoint Online Office 365

972. Are any governance changes sufficient to impact achievement?

973. How do you create a self-sustaining capacity for a collaborative culture?

974. Are any validation activities performed?

975. How is assessment information achieved, stored?

976. What are they responsible for?

977. To what degree can team members meet frequently enough to accomplish the teams ends?

978. Does the rater (supervisor) have to wait for the interim or final performance assessment review to tell an employee that the employees performance is unsatisfactory?

979. What are best practices in use for the performance measurement system?

980. To what degree can team members frequently and easily communicate with one another?

981. Why do performance reviews?

982. Does adaptive training work?

983. What is the Business Management Oversight Process?

984. What is a general description of the processes under performance measurement and assessment?

985. Who receives a benchmark visit?

986. What stakeholders must be involved in the development and oversight of the performance plan?

987. In what areas would you like to concentrate your knowledge and resources?

988. What is a significant fact or event?

989. For what period of time is a member rated?

3.10 Issue Log: SharePoint Online Office 365

990. What would have to change?

991. Who is the stakeholder?

992. What is the impact on the risks?

993. Do you feel more overwhelmed by stakeholders?

994. In classifying stakeholders, which approach to do so are you using?

995. What date was the issue resolved?

996. Do you have members of your team responsible for certain stakeholders?

997. How were past initiatives successful?

998. What is the stakeholders political influence?

999. Are there too many who have an interest in some aspect of your work?

1000. How is this initiative related to other portfolios, programs, or SharePoint Online Office 365 projects?

1001. Is the issue log kept in a safe place?

1002. Are you constantly rushing from meeting to meeting?

1003. What effort will a change need?

1004. Can you think of other people who might have concerns or interests?

1005. What does the stakeholder need from the team?

1006. Why do you manage human resources?

1007. Are stakeholder roles recognized by your organization?

4.0 Monitoring and Controlling Process Group: SharePoint Online Office 365

1008. Feasibility: how much money, time, and effort can you put into this?

1009. What areas were overlooked on this SharePoint Online Office 365 project?

1010. Who needs to be engaged upfront to ensure use of results?

1011. Is the program in place as intended?

1012. Were escalated issues resolved promptly?

1013. Is the verbiage used appropriate and understandable?

1014. Are the necessary foundations in place to ensure the sustainability of the results of the programme?

1015. How was the program set-up initiated?

1016. How can you make your needs known?

1017. Did you implement the program as designed?

1018. How is agile program management done?

1019. When will the SharePoint Online Office 365

project be done?

1020. Propriety: who needs to be involved in the evaluation to be ethical?

1021. Is there adequate validation on required fields?

1022. How well did the chosen processes produce the expected results?

1023. Is progress on outcomes due to your program?

4.1 Project Performance Report: SharePoint Online Office 365

1024. To what degree do team members agree with the goals, relative importance, and the ways in which achievement will be measured?

1025. How can SharePoint Online Office 365 project sustainability be maintained?

1026. To what degree is the team cognizant of small wins to be celebrated along the way?

1027. To what degree will team members, individually and collectively, commit time to help themselves and others learn and develop skills?

1028. To what degree do team members frequently explore the teams purpose and its implications?

1029. To what degree will the approach capitalize on and enhance the skills of all team members in a manner that takes into consideration other demands on members of the team?

1030. To what degree do team members feel that the purpose of the team is important, if not exciting?

1031. To what degree do team members articulate the teams work approach?

1032. What degree are the relative importance and priority of the goals clear to all team members?

1033. To what degree do the structures of the formal organization motivate taskrelevant behavior and facilitate task completion?

1034. To what degree can all members engage in open and interactive considerations?

1035. Next Steps?

1036. To what degree is there a sense that only the team can succeed?

1037. To what degree will the team adopt a concrete, clearly understood, and agreed-upon approach that will result in achievement of the teams goals?

1038. What is the degree to which rules govern information exchange between individuals within your organization?

4.2 Variance Analysis: SharePoint Online Office 365

1039. Is work progressively subdivided into detailed work packages as requirements are defined?

1040. How do you identify and isolate causes of favorable and unfavorable cost and schedule variances?

1041. When, during the last four quarters, did a primary business event occur causing a fluctuation?

1042. Did an existing competitor change strategy?

1043. What are the direct labor dollars and/or hours?

1044. What can be the cause of an increase in costs?

1045. Are data elements reconcilable between internal summary reports and reports forwarded to the stakeholders?

1046. What business event caused the fluctuation?

1047. Are there knowledgeable SharePoint Online Office 365 projections of future performance?

1048. Why are standard cost systems used?

1049. Does the contractors system provide unit or lot costs when applicable?

1050. What is the dollar amount of the fluctuation?

1051. Budgeted cost for work performed?

1052. How have the setting and use of standards changed over time?

1053. Are the actual costs used for variance analysis reconcilable with data from the accounting system?

1054. What types of services and expense are shared between business segments?

1055. Who is generally responsible for monitoring and taking action on variances?

1056. Are meaningful indicators identified for use in measuring the status of cost and schedule performance?

1057. How do you identify potential or actual overruns and underruns?

4.3 Earned Value Status: SharePoint Online Office 365

1058. Validation is a process of ensuring that the developed system will actually achieve the stakeholders desired outcomes; Are you building the right product? What do you validate?

1059. If earned value management (EVM) is so good in determining the true status of a SharePoint Online Office 365 project and SharePoint Online Office 365 project its completion, why is it that hardly any one uses it in information systems related SharePoint Online Office 365 projects?

1060. When is it going to finish?

1061. Where are your problem areas?

1062. How does this compare with other SharePoint Online Office 365 projects?

1063. Verification is a process of ensuring that the developed system satisfies the stakeholders agreements and specifications; Are you building the product right? What do you verify?

1064. Where is evidence-based earned value in your organization reported?

1065. Earned value can be used in almost any SharePoint Online Office 365 project situation and in almost any SharePoint Online Office 365 project environment. it may be used on large SharePoint Online Office 365 projects, medium sized SharePoint Online Office 365 projects, tiny SharePoint Online Office 365 projects (in cut-down form), complex and simple SharePoint Online Office 365 projects and in any market sector. some people, of course, know all about earned value, they have used it for years - but perhaps not as effectively as they could have?

1066. How much is it going to cost by the finish?

1067. What is the unit of forecast value?

1068. Are you hitting your SharePoint Online Office 365 projects targets?

4.4 Risk Audit: SharePoint Online Office 365

1069. Does your organization have or has considered the need for insurance covers: public liability, professional indemnity and directors and officers liability?

1070. Will participants be required to sign a legally counselled waiver or risk disclaimer when entering an event?

1071. Has risk management been considered when planning an event?

1072. Are formal technical reviews part of this process?

1073. To what extent are auditors influenced by the business risk assessment in the audit process, and how can auditors create more effective mental models to more fully examine contradictory evidence?

1074. Is an annual audit required and conducted of your financial records?

1075. Do you record and file all audits?

1076. Who audits the auditor?

1077. Are end-users enthusiastically committed to the SharePoint Online Office 365 project and the system/

product to be built?

1078. Are duties out-of-class?

1079. Are audit program plans risk-adjusted?

1080. Does your auditor understand your business?

1081. Have staff received necessary training?

1082. Is your organization an exempt employer for payroll tax purposes?

1083. For paid staff, does your organization comply with the minimum conditions for employment and/or the applicable modern award?

1084. Improving fraud detection: do auditors react to abnormal inconsistencies between financial and non-financial measures?

1085. Is your organization willing to commit significant time to the requirements gathering process?

1086. Do staff understand the extent of duty of care?

1087. How do you manage risk?

4.5 Contractor Status Report: SharePoint Online Office 365

1088. What are the minimum and optimal bandwidth requirements for the proposed solution?

1089. Who can list a SharePoint Online Office 365 project as organization experience, your organization or a previous employee of your organization?

1090. What was the budget or estimated cost for your organizations services?

1091. If applicable; describe your standard schedule for new software version releases. Are new software version releases included in the standard maintenance plan?

1092. How does the proposed individual meet each requirement?

1093. What was the final actual cost?

1094. How is risk transferred?

1095. What process manages the contracts?

1096. What was the actual budget or estimated cost for your organizations services?

1097. What was the overall budget or estimated cost?

1098. How long have you been using the services?

1099. What is the average response time for answering a support call?

1100. Are there contractual transfer concerns?

1101. Describe how often regular updates are made to the proposed solution. Are corresponding regular updates included in the standard maintenance plan?

4.6 Formal Acceptance: SharePoint Online Office 365

1102. Was the client satisfied with the SharePoint Online Office 365 project results?

1103. Did the SharePoint Online Office 365 project manager and team act in a professional and ethical manner?

1104. Did the SharePoint Online Office 365 project achieve its MOV?

1105. Who would use it?

1106. What is the Acceptance Management Process?

1107. Was the sponsor/customer satisfied?

1108. Do you buy-in installation services?

1109. Was business value realized?

1110. Was the SharePoint Online Office 365 project work done on time, within budget, and according to specification?

1111. Do you perform formal acceptance or burn-in tests?

1112. Does it do what SharePoint Online Office 365 project team said it would?

1113. Was the SharePoint Online Office 365 project managed well?

1114. Was the SharePoint Online Office 365 project goal achieved?

1115. Do you buy pre-configured systems or build your own configuration?

1116. Does it do what client said it would?

1117. Have all comments been addressed?

1118. What function(s) does it fill or meet?

1119. What are the requirements against which to test, Who will execute?

1120. What lessons were learned about your SharePoint Online Office 365 project management methodology?

1121. What can you do better next time?

5.0 Closing Process Group: SharePoint Online Office 365

1122. Did the SharePoint Online Office 365 project team have the right skills?

1123. Just how important is your work to the overall success of the SharePoint Online Office 365 project?

1124. Is the SharePoint Online Office 365 project funded?

1125. What can you do better next time, and what specific actions can you take to improve?

1126. When will the SharePoint Online Office 365 project be done?

1127. Did the SharePoint Online Office 365 project management methodology work?

1128. What were the actual outcomes?

1129. What is the risk of failure to your organization?

1130. Will the SharePoint Online Office 365 project deliverable(s) replace a current asset or group of assets?

1131. Based on your SharePoint Online Office 365 project communication management plan, what worked well?

1132. How will staff learn how to use the deliverables?

1133. What is the SharePoint Online Office 365 project Management Process?

1134. Is this a follow-on to a previous SharePoint Online Office 365 project?

1135. Were decisions made in a timely manner?

1136. How dependent is the SharePoint Online Office 365 project on other SharePoint Online Office 365 projects or work efforts?

1137. Mitigate. what will you do to minimize the impact should a risk event occur?

1138. Was the user/client satisfied with the end product?

1139. Does the close educate others to improve performance?

5.1 Procurement Audit: SharePoint Online Office 365

1140. Are all purchase orders reviewed by someone other than the individual preparing the purchase order (reasonableness of order and vendor selection)?

1141. Can changes be made to automatic disbursement programs without proper approval of management?

1142. Does the procurement SharePoint Online Office 365 project have a clear goal and does the goal meet the specified needs of the users?

1143. Was the outcome of the award process properly reached and communicated?

1144. Are internal control mechanisms performed before payments?

1145. Were technical requirements set strict enough to guarantee the desired performance without being unnecessarily tight to exclude favourable bids that do not comply with all requirements?

1146. Was the expert likely to gain privileged knowledge from his activity which could be advantageous for him in a subsequent competition?

1147. Is it calculated whether aggregated procurement can be more cost-efficient?

1148. Does the procurement SharePoint Online Office 365 project comply with European Communities regulations and rules?

1149. Are prices always included on the purchase order?

1150. Does the strategy discus the best manner of purchase, considering the types of goods and services needed?

1151. Are risks in the external environment identified, for example: Budgetary constraints?

1152. Are all pre-numbered checks accounted for on a regular basis?

1153. Did the chosen procedure ensure competition and transparency?

1154. Is there any objection?

1155. Are existing suppliers that have a special right to be consulted being contacted?

1156. Are regulations and protective measures in place to avoid corruption?

1157. Are procurement processes well organized and documented?

1158. Are the users needs clearly and invariably defined and has the expected outcome or mission been clearly identified and communicated in measurable terms?

1159. Did your organization decide upon an adequate and admissible procurement procedure?

5.2 Contract Close-Out: SharePoint Online Office 365

1160. Have all contract records been included in the SharePoint Online Office 365 project archives?

1161. Was the contract sufficiently clear so as not to result in numerous disputes and misunderstandings?

1162. Change in attitude or behavior?

1163. What happens to the recipient of services?

1164. Are the signers the authorized officials?

1165. Why Outsource?

1166. Parties: who is involved?

1167. Change in circumstances?

1168. Have all contracts been completed?

1169. Has each contract been audited to verify acceptance and delivery?

1170. Have all acceptance criteria been met prior to final payment to contractors?

1171. Parties: Authorized?

1172. Was the contract type appropriate?

1173. Was the contract complete without requiring numerous changes and revisions?

1174. How/when used ?

1175. How does it work?

1176. Have all contracts been closed?

1177. How is the contracting office notified of the automatic contract close-out?

1178. Change in knowledge?

1179. What is capture management?

5.3 Project or Phase Close-Out: SharePoint Online Office 365

1180. Planned remaining costs?

1181. Did the SharePoint Online Office 365 project management methodology work?

1182. What information is each stakeholder group interested in?

1183. What hierarchical authority does the stakeholder have in your organization?

1184. What was the preferred delivery mechanism?

1185. Were risks identified and mitigated?

1186. How often did each stakeholder need an update?

1187. What advantages do the an individual interview have over a group meeting, and vice-versa?

1188. Who is responsible for award close-out?

1189. Complete yes or no?

1190. Were the outcomes different from the already stated planned?

1191. What were the goals and objectives of the communications strategy for the SharePoint Online

Office 365 project?

1192. What is this stakeholder expecting?

1193. What was expected from each stakeholder?

1194. Who are the SharePoint Online Office 365 project stakeholders and what are roles and involvement?

1195. Who exerted influence that has positively affected or negatively impacted the SharePoint Online Office 365 project?

1196. What benefits or impacts does the stakeholder group expect to obtain as a result of the SharePoint Online Office 365 project?

1197. What stakeholder group needs, expectations, and interests are being met by the SharePoint Online Office 365 project?

5.4 Lessons Learned: SharePoint Online Office 365

1198. Where do you go from here?

1199. What skills did you need that were missing on this SharePoint Online Office 365 project?

1200. What was helpful to know when planning the deployment?

1201. Were cost budgets met?

1202. How do security constraints impact the case?

1203. How well defined were the acceptance criteria for SharePoint Online Office 365 project deliverables?

1204. What did you do right?

1205. Who is responsible for each action?

1206. To what extent was the evolution of risks communicated?

1207. Were the right people available when required?

1208. How does the budget cycle affect the case?

1209. What is the expected lifespan of the deliverable?

1210. What is the growth stage of the organization?

1211. What would you approach differently next time?

1212. What report generation capability is needed?

1213. Who had fiscal authority to manage the funding for the SharePoint Online Office 365 project, did that work?

1214. What were the major enablers to a quick response?

1215. What other questions should you have asked?

1216. Were the aims and objectives achieved?

1217. What are the performance measures?

Index

pressing   129
pressures   163
prevent   20, 49, 60, 62, 232
prevented   17
previous   34, 164, 250, 255
previously   135, 203, 224
prices 257
pricing 114
primarily   74
primary   100, 157, 244
principles   157
priorities   40
prioritize   40-41, 44
priority 42-43, 242
privacy   40, 79, 97
privileged   72, 256
probably   169
problem   16, 20, 23, 25, 27, 34-35, 42, 61-62, 140, 220, 227, 234, 246
problems   20, 65, 77, 190-191
procedure   106, 114, 116, 233, 257-258
procedures   10, 53, 78, 80, 82-83, 125, 154, 167, 176, 186, 210, 226, 233
proceed   201
process   1-4, 6-8, 10, 28, 30, 32, 34-35, 37, 40-42, 44-45, 49-54, 56-59, 61-62, 67, 70-71, 73, 77-82, 84, 86, 129-131, 136-137, 140, 142-143, 146, 148-151, 167, 172, 176, 186, 190-191, 203-204, 206, 210, 213-214, 218, 227, 230-232, 235, 237, 240, 246, 248-250, 252, 254-256
processed   58, 62
processes   33, 45, 51-54, 57-58, 60, 77, 129, 136, 186-187, 190, 219, 224, 233, 237, 241, 257
processing   50, 53, 57, 78
procuring   140
produce   167, 221, 241
producing   146
product   1, 101-102, 124, 131, 142, 163, 184, 186-187, 200, 205, 208, 220-221, 225, 231, 246, 249, 255
production   45, 99, 233
products   1, 83, 101-102, 132, 136, 142, 146, 181, 196, 214, 219-220, 225, 235
profit   188
profits 58

Lightning Source UK Ltd.
Milton Keynes UK
UKHW040910281119
354396UK00010B/1410/P